56

Charles Arn

Heartbeat!
How to Turn Passion into Ministry
in Your Church

Introducing **Side-Doors**—
Your Key to Effective Missional
Outreach in the 21st Century

PRESS

contents

introduction

KESWICK, UNITED KINGDOM (ANS) — Walking slowly to the podium, assisted by a cane and his research assistant, the theologian was met by a standing ovation from the overflow crowd on the warm summer evening of July 17th. Several years earlier TIME magazine had named him "One of the 100 most influential people on the planet." What would he say in his final address to those listening in that room and around the world?

John Stott began by recalling how perplexed he had been as a younger Christian, about the answer to the question, "What is God's purpose for His people?" In his message that night Stott described the resolution to his lifelong search:

"I want to share with you where my mind has come to rest as I approach the end of my pilgrimage on earth. Here it is: God wants His people to become like Christ. *Christ-likeness is the will of God for the people of God.*"[1]

Stott spent the rest of the evening addressing this matter of incarnational evangelism; a process, he noted, "that can turn the world upside down." Stott's simple definition of incarnational evangelism was: *"Entering into other people's worlds with Christ-likeness."*[2] Incarnational evangelism, said Stott, is the road the church must walk in the 21st century. Our evangelistic efforts often lead to failure, he observed, simply because we don't act like the Christ we proclaim. Quoting John Poulton, Stott noted that, "The most effective preaching comes from those who embody their message. What communicates now are not words or ideas, but rather personal authenticity; that is, Christ-likeness."

In two words, that is what this book is about: Incarnational Evangelism. We will present an effective, proven, yet very enjoyable way for those in your church to enter into other people's worlds with contagious Christ-likeness. Some call this the "missional approach", others "externally-focused." In its simplest form, incarnational evangelism is what the Christian life should be all about—becoming more like Christ in this world.

But after this Introduction, I would like to say goodbye to the term "incarnational evangelism." That's because what we'll be sharing in this book is a process for laypeople...who don't get all that jazzed with big theological terms. Rather, we'll be using words like "side-doors," and "heartbeat," and "passion," and "fun." Words that more accurately describe the process we will be exploring.

This book is not necessarily about the "what" or "why" of incarnational evangelism, as much as the "how." We'll be talking about riding motorcycles, about finding jobs, about dealing with cancer, and about dancing the hula! And how the people in your church can respond to Christ's command to "...go and make disciples," while having the time of their lives!

Where Do We Be Christ-like?

A closer look at how Jesus' command was given, in the original Greek, gives us an insight into how he wants us to carry it out. The word "go", when Jesus said "...go and make disciples," is more correctly translated to mean: "as you are going". In other words, Jesus was not saying drop everything, pack your bags and go off to a foreign land. He was saying that as you are going...as you are participating in your world…as you are involved in your normal everyday encounters with people…in that context, make disciples.

That is the process of incarnational evangelism. And, while Stott is right, that it has the power to turn the world upside down, incarnational evangelism also has the power to turn your local church upside down. And your community. The encouraging news is that you don't have to be a mega-church to do it. While most mega-churches are, in fact, practicing incarnational evangelism, they don't have a corner on the idea, or the needs in your community to which your church members can respond like Christ. There are hundreds of possible ways and places for your people to become incarnational evangelists in your community. And, in this book, we will show you a practical, proven way to do so. It's a process Nelson Searcy calls, "putting wheels on the missional wagon."

The Silver Bullet for Making Disciples

Wikipedia defines *silver bullet* as: "Any straightforward solution perceived to have extreme effectiveness; a phrase that typically appears with an expectation that a new practice or technology will cure a major prevailing problem."[3]

Based on my 30+ years in studying the process of evangelism and church growth, I can confidently say there is a "silver bullet" for fulfilling Christ's command to go and make disciples. Here it is:

The most effective evangelism—by far—occurs through meaningful relationships between Christians and non-Christians.

Did you know that over twice as many non-Christians come to Christ through relationships with Christian friends or relatives than all other reasons—combined?[4]

Many times in his ministry Jesus talked about and modeled this "disciple-making silver bullet." To the demon-possessed man (Mark 5:19) he said, "go home to your friends and tell them what wonderful things God has done for you..." When Zacchaeus believed, Christ told him that salvation had also come to his friends and family (Luke 19:9). After Jesus healed the son of a royal official we learn that he, and all of his family and friends, believed (Mark 2:14-15). Jesus was teaching about sharing God's love with the people we already know. It is *the way* the Gospel travels!

In your next devotion time look up that word "household" in your Bible concordance. You will find it not only in the references above, but in many other verses, as well. In the original Greek, the word is *oikos*, and it has a fascinating meaning. *Oikos* referred to the people in a person's social network.[5] It included a person's immediate family (father, brother, wife, etc.). It included a person's extended family (cousin, brother-in-law, grandparent, nephew, etc.). *Oikos* referred to the servants that stayed in the living compound of the first century home. It referred to the servants' families who also lived there. The word *oikos* referred to a person's close friends, as well as their work associates. When the tremendous earthquake caused the Philippian jailer to desperately cry out: "What must I do to be saved?" Paul responded, "Believe on the Lord Jesus Christ and you will be saved... you and your *oikos*" (Acts 16:31). Michael Green observes, "The early Christians knew that when the message of faith was heard and demonstrated by friends and family who were known and trusted...receptivity to the Gospel increased tremendously."[6]

Existing relationships have been the primary means by which the Gospel has traveled from the first century church right up to today. Donald McGavran, the early pioneer in the study of church growth, wrote one of his first books titled, *The Bridges of God*.[7] In it he explained how the Gospel has timelessly crossed over the "bridges" of existing relationships between believer and unbeliever. Research still shows that it is through the natural existing relationships of believers with non-believers that the Gospel continues to spread most effectively.[8]

So, incarnational evangelism is simply being intentionally Christ-like in our normal, everyday life — with the people in our social network.

A Problem with Shooting the Silver Bullet

But, there is one essential requirement for being an incarnational evangelist: *we must be close enough to unbelievers for Christ to be observed and experienced in us.* And there's the rub. The problem is that the longer we are in church, the more friends we have who are also in our church…and the fewer friends we have who are outside the church. Let me repeat this important problem-statement, because it is one of the major obstacles to the spread of the Christian Gospel today: *Most Christians have very few close friends who are non-Christian.* Without such relationships, it is impossible to be Christ-like. Remember Stott's definition of incarnational evangelism? Entering into other people's worlds with Christ-likeness. And this does not mean other Christians' worlds.

So, how do we enter into a non-Christian's world to be Christ-like if we don't really know any non-Christians? The answer is easy. We need to become more like Jesus — we need friends who are "…tax collectors and sinners!" (Matt. 11:19) Or, if you prefer Eugene Peterson's version, Jesus was spoken of as "…a friend of the riffraff."

The average new Christian can list 12-13 non-believing friends and relatives in his/her social network[9]. But a curious thing begins to happen the longer we are Christians. Each year we can list fewer and fewer non-Christians in our social community. It's not that our friends and relatives all become Christians, although this sometimes happens. Rather, it is a phenomena Donald McGavran called "redemption and lift."[10] The more we learn about Christ, and the more we want to become like Christ, the more comfortable we are around people on this same faith journey. Some of us long-time believers, in fact, have gotten to the point where we have *no* close friends or relatives outside the church.

One reason that 85+% of today's churches are not growing is that the social networks of people in these churches are almost entirely within the church. Worse yet, most churches actually program to encourage this relational isolation. Church activities are geared toward existing members. "Successful" events are when a high percentage of members attend. Small groups are formed primarily for church attenders. As a result, not only do church members have few non-Christian people with whom they associate... non-Christian people in the community have few or no close friends in the church!

From Christ's point of view, I believe, this is a serious problem. How can Christ's missional task be accomplished if His people are not in the world? "My prayer," said Jesus to His Father, "is not that you take them [Christ's followers] out of the world, but that you protect them from the evil one" (John 17:15). In fact, Christians are *supposed* to be in the world, just not of the world. Paul knew that he needed to connect with "the riffraff" before he could communicate with them:

> *I didn't take on their way of life. I kept my bearings in Christ. But I entered their world and tried to experience things from their point of view. I've become just about every sort of servant there is in my attempts to lead those I meet into a God-saved life. I did all this because of the Message. I didn't just want to talk about it; I wanted to be in on it!"* (I Cor. 9:19-23 The Message)

We are to be the salt of the earth (Matt. 5:13). And salt does not season itself.

But like the wall that divided the German people and eventually created two separate cultures, there are walls that isolate many Christians from non-Christians today. "Doors" that could allow people to pass through these relational walls, simply do not exist.

The Solution to the Problem

The solution is what this book is all about. It is to help you and your church knock holes in those walls that separate your church from the people in your community. I call those holes, "side-doors." As we will see, side-doors are a proven and exciting way to build relationships with unchurched people. Side-doors are how people *inside* your church can genuinely connect with people in your neighborhood, and how people *outside* your church can experience real Christian community through contact with members of the body of Christ.

Sound impossible? Not only is it possible...it is happening. Such ministries are the "frontier topic" for understanding the world's most effective churches.[11] And, in this book I want to share with you how it can happen in *your* church. If I were introducing a new outreach idea or program in these pages, I might be more concerned as to whether I could make good on a promise of more people in your church involved in outreach, doing ministry, and genuinely enjoying it. But these are not new ideas...at least to the churches that are already doing it.

Organization of this Book

Heartbeat! How to Turn Passion Into Ministry is organized into three sections: PART ONE: The Power of Side-doors, PART TWO: How to Start a Heartbeat Ministry, and PART THREE: Bring Life to Your Hearbeats.

Here is a brief description of each:

PART ONE: The Power of Side-Doors. "Side-Doors" is truly a great idea! It combines the best of today's missional thinking with Christ's eternal concern for the growth of His Church. More and more churches are actually seeing their "side-doors" become the primary source of their new members. And, what really excites me is that you don't need to be a mega-church to build side-doors (although you can be). You don't even need to be a medium-sized church to start side-doors (although you can be). Churches of even 10 people can build effective side-doors that connect with and successfully reach into their community.

In Part One we'll talk about what side-doors are—and what they aren't. We'll look at how and why missional side-doors are the key to effective disciple-making in the 21st century. And, in the last chapter of Part One, we will introduce "Heartbeat Ministry"—the way to turn your church members' various interests and passions into effective side-doors.

PART TWO: How to Start a Heartbeat Ministry. Building side-doors is not the pastor's job. Side-doors grow out of the passion of lay people in a church. The chapters in Part Two provide a step-by-step "blueprint" for starting a successful new ministry. The group, class, club, or activity that grows out of their heartbeat will allow members to develop deep and meaningful relationships with people of similar heartbeats in your community, which become well-traveled side-doors to Christ and your church.

PART THREE: Bring Life to Your Heartbeats. Much of this book has come from my last eight years of research and testing of side-door ministries. In the process, I've learned things that will save you some frustration and make your side-doors most successful. One discovery, for example, was the value of a "Ministry Coach." If you are planning to build missional side-doors into your community, you will want to have a ministry coach. Chapter Fifteen and Sixteen provide a kind of job description for this person(s). He/she may be a layperson or staff member...full-time or part-time...paid or volunteer. In the side-door metaphor, the ministry coach is the "general contractor." He/she understands and oversees the exciting process of constructing effective new side-doors in your church.

So, Are You Ready to Start Building?

You may be in a church that has been plateaued or declining in recent years. I believe incarnational evangelism—practiced through creating missional side-doors—can be your key to effective new outreach and congregational growth.

Perhaps you are in the 15% of churches that are already seeing growth in worship attendance. A side-door building strategy will help you shift into overdrive to accelerate the number of people reached through your church.

Perhaps you feel that the "missional renaissance" going on in churches today has merit and you want your congregation to become more missional in its focus and priorities. A side-door building strategy is your answer to the question, *"Where do we start?"*

Well, actually, you have already started. And, as you continue through this book, you will find a very practical, step-by-step approach to practicing incarnational evangelism in your community. This process comes from research of many churches that are doing it successfully. It comes from pilot projects where we have tested the process. And it comes from the observation that "side-doors" are a proven way to "knock holes" in the walls separating so many churches from so many people outside.

I really think you're going to enjoy this...

Part One

Discover the Power of "Side-Doors"

chapter one

Side-Doors:
What They Are...
and Why You Need Them

The prescription for growing a church is simple: *More people must come in than go out.*

But *experiencing* positive people flow is not quite as simple. In fact, over 85% of Protestant churches are not.

As a church consultant for over 30 years, I have come to a sobering conclusion: The "front doors" of most churches are closing. There are fewer people visiting churches, and fewer visitors are staying. Let me re-state this important point: Hundreds of thousands of churches in America have an insufficient number of visitors coming in their "front doors" to make up for those who are leaving out the "back doors." As a result, churches that continue to rely on visitors as their primary source of prospects...will die within a few generations.

"Once upon a time, not so long ago," observes George Hunter, noted researcher, "churches relied on two 'front doors' for reaching people: the worship service and the Sunday School. Today, the most apostolic congregations reach even more people through 'side doors'..."[1]

Perhaps you have heard the term "side-doors" applied to the church. It's not a new idea, certainly not a complex one. But increasingly, it is a critical idea for church leaders to understand. Side-doors are a powerful way to harness the passion and energy in a church, and channel it into effective outreach. Side-doors have the potential to connect with—and reach—many new people in a community for Jesus Christ and His Church.

What are Side Doors?

I have asked Rev. Todd Pridemore, minister of outreach at a medium-sized church in Columbia, Missouri to tell us about his church's side-doors. In three short stories you will see the exciting opportunities for ministry and outreach that side-doors provide. You'll get the idea pretty quickly. As Todd, and a growing number of church leaders will tell you, building side-doors in your church will dramatically increase the number of people in your community who will touch the face of Jesus...

"A couple of years ago, a woman in our congregation sensed a calling to invite a friend and her family to church. However, the church member knew it was very unlikely that this unchurched family would respond to her invitation to attend the Sunday morning worship service. The woman's children participated in an outreach-oriented basketball league at the church, so she invited the parents to involve their two children in that activity, as well. The kids enrolled in the basketball program, and everyone loved the experience. Nearly two years later, three of their four previously unchurched family members were baptized as new members of our church.

"Another church member, a young father, met a new neighbor who did not attend any church in the community. The neighbor had moved to this area from another state and had virtually no friends nearby. Although he grew up as a Catholic, he did not consider religion and spirituality

*to be a significant part of his life. The church member took
advantage of a fishing tournament sponsored by our church
as a way to involve his new friend. After participating in
two fishing tournaments over a period of four months, the
neighbor began attending a Bible discussion group. He now
attends church regularly, where he is exploring Christianity
in ways he never has before.*

*"Still another church member, a young woman, worked
with a young lady who had not gone to church since childhood. The church member talked with her co-worker about
church and other religious issues, occasionally inviting her
to attend some of the "less threatening" activities at the
church, such as social events and women's activities. After
months of being invited, the co-worker finally attended a
women's brunch at the church and enjoyed it immensely.
After several more months of church-related conversations
and invitations, the young lady finally attended a Sunday
morning worship service. This woman felt God's presence
through the worship service, as well as through the relationships she had developed with her co-worker and others at
the church. She felt compelled to investigate Christian faith
on a deeper level, and she was recently baptized."*

These three stories focus on the lives of previously
unchurched people who did not come into that church through
their "front door." Their first contact was not in the worship
service or Sunday school hour. In fact, Todd is convinced
that had the front doors been the only way to get into their
church, these people would likely not be involved today.
Instead, these—and thousands of other people in churches
around the country—came to Christ and the church through
"side-doors."

Side-door: A church-sponsored program, group, or
activity in which a non-member can become comfort-

ably involved on a regular basis. An ongoing function in which the non-member can develop meaningful and valued relationships with people in the church.

Goal of an Effective Side-door: To provide an opportunity for participants (church members and non-members) to develop friendships around something important that they share in common.

Here are just a few examples of actual side-doors that churches have created where members and non-members are developing friendships around common interests. There are side-doors in churches for people who:

> • *ride motorcycles* • *have children in the military* • *own RVs* • *are recent widowers* • *are newlyweds* • *enjoy reading books* • *are unemployed* • *suffer from chronic pain* • *have husbands in jail* • *are nominal Jews* • *have spouses who are not believers* • *are fishermen* • *are single mothers* • *want to get in better physical condition* • *wish to help homeless families* • *play softball* • *are interested in end-times* • *have a bed-ridden parent* • *are raising grandchildren* • *are moms with teenage daughters* • *need help managing their finances* • *enjoy scrap-booking* • *are children in blended families* • *have children with a learning disability* • *are married to men who travel frequently* • *enjoy radio controlled airplanes* • *are pregnant* • *are affected by homosexuality* • *struggle with chemical dependency* • *are empty-nesters* • *enjoy camping* • *are divorced with no children* • *have a family member diagnosed with cancer* • *are single dads* • *enjoy SCUBA diving* • *are hearing-impaired* ...**and that's just a start!**

The idea of providing a place for unchurched people to connect with Christians *before* they become active church participants—or even Christ-followers—has actually been around for a while. John Wesley, the early religious pioneer, insisted on using side-doors in his evangelistic ministry, as we read in the book *To Spread the Power…*

"Wesley had three ultimate objectives for people: 1) that they experience the grace of God and the gift of faith, and become conscious followers of Jesus Christ; 2) that they be "united" with others in a "class" and a "society" [i.e., be involved with a group of believers]; 3) that upon achievement of 1 and 2, they experience growth toward Christian perfection. It is crucial to point out that the first two objectives could be achieved in a person's life-history in either order, and the more usual sequence was, 2, 1.

"That is, most of the people who became Methodist converts first joined a class or group [a side-door], and sometime later became conscious Christians! This helps to explain why Wesley, in his extensive open-air field preaching, never invited people to accept Jesus Christ and become Christians on the spot! That statement must surely shock those of us whose assumptions about public evangelism have been carved out in the Billy Graham era, as it would shock the evangelical Christians of any generation since Charles Grandison Finney first began inviting responders to what he called the 'mourner's bench'."[2]

Some two hundred fifty years after Wesley began the Methodist Church, Rev. Kwasi Kena, Director of Evangelism Ministries for the United Methodist Church, observed: "In

order to proliferate, we must provide more 'side door' opportunities for entry into the life of our churches."[3]

From a trends perspective, side-doors are definitely on the
way in. According to Lyle Schaller, widely respected church
observer, most of today's regular church attenders who were
born before 1935 made their initial contact with their church
on Sunday morning through the front door. However, a large
proportion of today's churchgoers who were born after 1935
made their initial contact through a side-door.[4]

Gary McIntosh suggests that about 10% of the churches
in the United States are side-door churches in which "...
most of the new people who connect with the church made
first contact through a ministry other than the worship service."[5] I have not tried to correlate Gary's 10% figure with
the fact that only about 14% of the churches in America
today are growing in worship attendance. But, from my
experience, I would not be surprised to find a high corre-
lation between side-door churches and growing churches.
Rev. Craig Williford, recalling his experience in leading two
growing emergent churches, says: "Our weekend services
were very vital. But the side door ministries produced more
evangelism and brought far more people into our church."[6]

Why Side-doors?

There are some good reasons why I hope you will choose
to enhance your church's ministry and outreach through
side-doors...

More people will be reached. The most important function
of a side-door is to extend God's love to people who would
most likely never attend a church on their own.

A popular topic of discussion these days is the difference
between "atrractional churches" and "missional churches."
The "attractional" approach to outreach, practiced in
American churches for years, involves three basic steps:

1) promoting church events to "seekers", 2) hoping for visitors, and 3) encouraging those visitors stay. The attractional approach can be an effective way to identify and connect with people who are interested and receptive. However, as our culture becomes less and less Christian, fewer people are taking the initiative to attend church-sponsored events. As noted earlier, for more and more churches the attractional model of depending on front-door visitors is not enough to replace the back-door departures of people leaving through death, transfer, and inactivity.

A new approach to outreach—the "missional" approach—is gaining influence as a means for helping non-Christian people experience God's love. This type of outreach assumes that the people of God are called to demonstrate Christ-likeness *in their community,* not waiting for their community to come to church.[7] As more Christians are incarnational in their worlds, more people will experience—and be attracted to—the love of God.

George Hunter notes that effective churches are actually practicing both attractional and missional outreach: "... a) they discover and invite all the people they can find who could be served through the church's present range of ministries; and b) they develop new outreach ministries to serve and reach additional populations. Some churches now feature 50 or more lay-led outreach ministries, and they are unstoppable local movements.[8]

Side-doors focus on the "b" in Hunter's list. They will help your church be more "missional" by creating new outreach ministries to serve and reach additional people groups in your community. While front doors are how people *come* to your church...side-doors are how your church *goes* to people. Side-doors are one of the best ways to "be my witnesses...to the ends of the earth" (Acts 1:8).

More kinds of people will be reached. Churches often tend
to be rather homogenous. Everyone seems to look the same,
sound the same, and talk the same. And the outreach potential is limited to others who look, sound, and talk the same
as they do.

But when you begin creating new side-doors into your
church, not only will the number of your people connections grow, but the *variety* of connections will grow, as well.
"The more affinity and sub-affinity groups you have in your
church," says David Williamson, on staff at Saddleback
Community Church, "the more effective the church will be
at reaching out to neighbors. Why? When you have groups
for particular ages, languages, and other micro-communi-
ties, you increase the chance that people will find a group
that fits them. Each affinity and sub-affinity group will reach
different kinds of people."[9]

The variety of side-door possibilities manifests itself in
many ways: common interests, common marital status, life-
issues, family types, common dreams of their future, hobbies, passions. Churches often experience even more growth
from such side-doors than they expected. For instance, a
church that begins a ministry with deaf people may find they
are also reaching the families of deaf people AND many
other people who are attracted to a church that cares enough
to minister to deaf people.[10] Several years from now, after
creating a number of new side-doors, you will look around
your church and see people who represent a much greater
diversity of age, marital status, family status, culture, interests, concerns, and needs of people...most of whom came
through your side-doors.

More members will be involved. A recent survey by REV!
Magazine found the assumption that 20% of the people in
church do 80% of the work is optimistic. It's even fewer.[11]
People do what they like to do. And if there's nothing they

like to do…they do nothing. Creating side-doors based around people's existing interests, priorities, and passions eliminates the greatest volunteer recruiting obstacle—motivation. When people are already motivated, you don't need to worry about creating it, just you need to figure how to channel it!

Here is a helpful continuum that illustrates why people do things.[12] Ask yourself, "how do we motivate people in our church?" In many churches, unfortunately, the tendency is toward the left end of the scale rather than the right.

Duress/ Force	Coercion	Duty	Obligation	Expectation	Desire	Personal Fulfillment	Love

Low Motivation   High Motivation

The common approach to lay ministry is for church leaders to promote an institutional agenda: "Come join this group…" "Please volunteer for that program…" "You'll want to attend those meetings…" Such tactics seek to direct people from whatever they really care about…to what the church leaders *think* they should care about. In contrast, creating side-door ministries *direct* people's interests…rather than try to *re-direct* them.

For example, a woman at Frazer Memorial United Methodist Church in Montgomery, Alabama learned that when premature babies are born in Montgomery's several hospitals, the hospital and parents often cannot find clothing for their three-pound baby; apparently no clothing manufacturer serves that small market. The woman was encouraged to organize a team of women who love to sew. They now sew the booties, gowns, and caps for every premature baby born in any hospital in Montgomery. They take the clothing to the hospitals, and they minister to anxious families. While the ministry has no strings attached, many families of "preemies" have joined Frazer Church, some as new Christians.[13]

More members will be involved in outreach. Simply having more people involved in church activities is no guarantee of more people reached for Christ. *What* they are doing is at least as important as *whether* they are doing.

Donald McGavran, in his significant work *Understanding Church Growth*,[14] provides a helpful way to evaluate the strategic deployment of laypersons in ministry. He calls them "Classes of Leaders." The two most important, for our purposes, are "Class I" and "Class II". "Class I" leaders are those people whose time and energy focus on *maintaining the existing church*. These people serve as deacons, teachers, ushers, greeters, choir members, elders, etc.. As McGavran says, "They are good people. They are God's people. The church would be a poor place without them. But, there is very little direct relationship between Class I activities and the actual growth of the church."[15]

"Class II" workers are those people whose time and energy focus outward *beyond* the walls of the church. They interact with people who are not part of the church and build connections with people in the community. The relationship between Class II roles and church growth is direct and causal.

The typical non-growing church has a Class I to Class II ratio of approximately 95:5. That is, for every 100 people involved in some sort of church ministry, 95% are in Class I—maintenance—roles. The good news is that building new side-doors will increase the number of people in your church involved in Class II activities. And that will increase conversion growth.

More groups will be started. Here's an equation you can take to the bank: *"new groups=new growth"*. In the *Church Growth Ratio Book* we suggest a "New Group Ratio" of 1:5. This means one of every five groups sponsored by your church (20%) should have been started in the previous two years.[16]

Why is there a direct relationship between new groups and new growth? Every group has a "saturation point." Like a sponge that cannot hold any more water, groups get to a point where they cannot hold any more members. I have found that approximately 90% of all groups saturate after two years. Beyond this point it becomes increasingly difficult for newcomers to "break into" the old group. Relationships have developed among the existing group members, experiences have been shared, trust has deepened, and the sense of community has developed to where newcomers are relationally "left out." It's not intentional. But it happens. And it's real.

The secret for dealing with this normal phenomena of group saturation is: *start new groups*. New side-door groups, in particular, address two key requirements for a healthy church: 1) the need for new groups, and 2) the need for new groups that include non-members. Side-door groups begin on a topic of common interest...involve churched and unchurched participants...and nurture relationships that often last a lifetime. And it is these relationships with God's people that often become the starting point to a relationship with God, himself.

More members will invite friends. Churches grow when friends bring friends. The antithesis is also true: churches don't grow when friends don't bring friends.

"We provide numerous 'side-door' ministries that give our members the opportunity to bring friends into contact with the church family," says Anthony J. Casoria, pastor of Center Grove Presbyterian Church (Edwardsville, Illinois). With more than a dozen side-doors already going, he says: "Additional side-door ministries and activities are added as

the Lord raises up members with the calling and commitment to implement and lead them."[17]

The typical church member will more likely invite a
friend to a side-door activity than she will invite that same
friend to a Sunday service. However, a fascinating thing
happens when the friend begins participating in a side-door
group. She makes other friends in that group, many of whom
attend the church. Then, when a special church activity or
Sunday service is planned, the chances are excellent that: 1)
the non-member will be invited to the event, and 2) the non-
member will attend with friends from the group. Remember
Todd Pridemore's three stories where this exact pattern happened in his church.

More new members will stay. Most pastors know the unfor-
tunate reality that not all new members become active members. Why do some leave, while others stay? Lyle Schaller
tells us:

> "Among those not related by kinship to a congrega-
> tion, those most likely to become active members
> are those who become part of a group, and develop
> meaningful relationships with others in that group,
> *before* formally uniting with that congregation. They
> are assimilated before they join."[18]

That is exactly why people who come to a church
through a side-door have a higher assimilation rate—they
have developed meaningful relationships with others, found
a sense of belonging, acceptance, and value in their side-door
group *before* they joined! Often, even, before they became
a believer. "We don't worry about people dropping out of
church who are connected to a small group," says the pastor
of a 15,000+ member church. "We know that those people
have been effectively assimilated."[19]

Your church's community visibility will increase. Churches
with high public exposure (at least the good kind) have more
walk-in visitors. So, what gives a church high public exposure? The media. How does a church get media exposure?
By doing something newsworthy.

Most side-door groups and functions, particularly ones
related to issues of current interest, are newsworthy. Local
newspapers and television stations will often feature church
activities that positively affect the local community. Several
years ago, for example, Fourth Presbyterian Church in
Chicago purchased property in the infamous Cabrini-Green
community. They decided to transform the Chicago Avenue
site into a cooperative garden, as a way to develop relationship with the families in Cabrini.[20] This side-door has
received much media coverage and increased the visitor
traffic to the church as a result. People-helping-people ministries get noticed. And many side-doors are just that.

Dependency on your facility will decrease. If your church
building is over 25 years old, chances are good that the
building is affecting your growth...negatively. Church
buildings can be growth-restricting obstacles.[21] It's a bad
sign when a visitor walks into your facility and the architec-
ture, alone, makes her feel uncomfortable. Side-door groups
don't have to (and sometimes shouldn't) meet in the church
facility. Rather, the people-connections are happening in the
community; in the "real world."

***You will move from a single-cell church to multi-cell
church.*** Half of the churches in the U.S. are under 80 in
attendance. They are single-cell churches, and stuck at the
most difficult barrier for any church to break.

A single-cell church is where community, fellowship,
caring, and spiritual growth occur when the entire congregation is together. Sociologically, a church cannot grow

beyond 100± without newcomers encountering a seemingly impenetrable group of people.

But when the sense of community, fellowship, caring, and spiritual growth begin to occur in the smaller units of the church—when the church begins to move from a single-cell organism to a multi-cell organism—the potential for growth increases dramatically. Side-door groups are tailor-made to facilitate the metamorphis from a single-cell to a multi-cell church.

Your church will not be dependent on walk-in visitors. In Chapter Two we will show how to calculate whether you have enough Sunday visitors to grow. But, as we have noted, most churches don't have enough. People who become part of a side-door group, however, develop friendships with people in your church. And those new friendships with church members greatly increase the likelihood of their visiting other church-related events and becoming part of your faith community.

The Risks

Obviously there are many good reasons to consider building new side-doors from your church to your community. "The best churches and denominations encourage new ministries," says Don Cousins.[22]

But you may be wondering about potential risks in committing to a strategy of side-doors. Let me briefly give you three...

1. A commitment to building side-doors will mean more connections with unchurched people than you have probably had for some time. The implication of these new relationships may not always be comfortable to members who have a "church is for us" mentality.

2. A commitment to building side-doors will mean that some of your members now involved in Class I (institutional maintenance) roles will be attracted to Class II (community outreach) activities. The implication of these ministry re-commitments may not always be comfortable to members who have a "church is for us" mentality.

3. A commitment to building side-doors will mean that members who are involved in beginning a new ministry (side-door) will need more freedom and flexibility than your church may be used to giving to members. The implication of this new freedom may not always be comfortable to members who have a "church is for us" mentality.

After it's all said and done, however, if you were to ask Jesus what His priorities are for your church, he would probably respond the same way he did to the man whom he just healed: ...go and tell your friends and neighbors what wonderful things God has done for you (Mark 5:19).

The simple rule is this: *The more doors you provide into the Christian faith community, the more people will walk through them.*

chapter two

Is It Really a Side-Door?

Aren't most church groups and activities side-doors? Or, at least potential side doors? After all, visitors are always welcome—and often invited—to most church functions. So, what really is a side-door, and what isn't?

Remember high school chemistry and those little pieces of litmus paper...the blue paper turned red in the presence of acid, and the red turned blue in a base solution? Well, there is a litmus test for side-doors. Here are eight essential ingredients in a side-door ministry. *Each* must exist for the activity to be an effective side-door. If all are not present, the activity may still be a helpful and important part of your church. But it is not a side-door, and will not increase your outreach in the same measure as a legitimate side-door. An important goal of this book is to help you build each of these ingredients into your side-doors. But for now, here's the test...

1. Side-doors involve members and non-members.

This is the most important one. The word "involve" is key. It does not simply mean "open" to outsiders. Nearly everything we do in the church is "open" to outsiders. Rather, a genuine side-door activity is *planned*, *programmed*, and *evaluated* around the assumption that church attenders and non-attenders will both be present.

After a side-door activity is concluded, one of the first questions should be: "How many unchurched people were there?" If the answer is "none," the discouragement should be as great as if the same answer were given to the question: "How many people were there?" In other words, if there are no contacts or connections with unchurched people at a side-door activity it is a failure, no matter how many church members show up.

Donald McGavran, founder of the modern church growth movement, was once asked: "Can small groups help the church grow?" Here was his response:

> Small groups do promote friendship, love, harmony, mutual support. All those things are desirable. However, if the small group consists exclusively of people who are already Christians, exclusively of the existing members of the church, then it has very little meaning for the growth of the church. On the other hand, if the small group makes it a point to include within itself those who have not accepted Christ, then the small group is probably one of the most effective ways of winning other people to Christ.[1]

Based on my observation of successful side-door ministries, I suggest a churched-to-unchurched ratio of *at least* 75:25. That is, no more than 75% of the side-door group are members of your church, and no less than 25% are non-members. A better ratio is 66:33. An ideal ratio is 50:50.

When evaluating your church groups and activities, use the following continuum to determine whether it is a potential side-door:

Participants in Church-related Activities

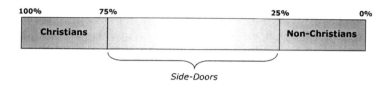

Side-Doors

Many church activities are comprised primarily of Christians and church attenders: Sunday School and adult Bible classes, small groups, men and women's fellowships, church dinners. All nice events. But not really side-doors, since they are not a major source of new connections with new people.

On the other hand, some churches mistakenly think that community groups using their facilities are side-doors. For example, the following quote is from the website of a church in Roseville, Minnesota: *"Our side-door ministries are various groups from the surrounding community that use our facility and provide opportunities for us to serve their needs: Chinese Day Care, Over-Eaters Anonymous, Alcoholics Anonymous, Clatterers Anonymous, Red Cross Blood Mobile, Home School Writing Project, Bonsai Society, Scottish Dancers, and Lions Club."*[2]

It is nice that this church would make their facilities available. And certainly the topics are the kind of special interests that *could* be exceptional side-doors. But based on my experience, I am fairly certain that these groups simply use the church's facilities, and make little or no contribution to the growth (if there is any) of that church.

Can an existing group in your church become a side-door? My response is: probably not. When a group has been together for years, it is nearly impossible for a significant number of newcomers to later become involved in that group, especially if they are unchurched newcomers. In the previous chapter we spoke of a group's saturation point.

Approximately 50% of all groups stop growing after one year, and 90% after two years. Certainly it is possible—and desirable—for existing groups to invite newcomers. And any group should be happy to receive new members. But side-doors have a significant number (at least 25%) of unchurched people involved in the group *from the outset*. Rather than try to force existing groups to become side-doors, it is far better to begin a new group or activity intentionally designed to be a side-door ministry.

As you read through the remaining characteristics of side-doors, you will see that many of the groups in your church meet the criteria. That is why this first one is so critical—there must be a *significant number (at least 25%) of unchurched people involved.*

2. Side-doors bring together people who share one or more important things in common.

There are several key ideas here; the obvious one is: "things in common." We all gravitate toward people with whom we share things in common. Think about your friends. Chances are you have a number of things in common. Affinity provides us with things to talk about together, places to go together, things to do together. Marriage counselors tell us the more things a couple has in common, the more likely they will be friends, enjoy their times together, and develop a strong, life-long relationship. "People connect most naturally with others who are like them," observed the pastor of a church that thrives around side-door ministries. "Common interests, ideas, studies, practices, hardships...these make the best framework for relational connectivity."[3]

Effective side-doors involve people who share things in common; and the more things they have in common, the better. For example, compare these two groups and imagine in which group members will have more to talk about and bond around: 1) a group for women, 2) a group for young single moms facing financial difficulties. One common denominator, compared to four!

Another key word in this criteria for a side-door is the word "important." Ask someone the question: "What are the important things that define who you are?" Then listen to how they describe themselves. Some of their descriptors are aspects which they have consciously chosen: a career, a hobby, a place to live. Other definers, however, are beyond their control: a child with Down's Syndrome, being unemployed, single parenthood. Important things about all of us are sometimes positive, sometimes not so. But they are who we are. And when we are with others who have similarly important things in their life, there's a connection. C. S. Lewis gives us a great insight about relationships: "Friendship is born at that moment when one person says to another: "What! You, too? I thought I was the only one."[4]

"Important" will likely fall into one or more of the following categories:

- *Age*
- *Marital Status*
- *Family Status*
- *Interest or Hobby*
- *Need, Concern, or Problem*
- *Religious Background or Attitude*
- *Cultural or Ethnic Identity*

In my research of church side-doors, I have found that most can be grouped into one of two categories: "Recreational" and "Support". But within these two areas, the interests and passions in a church are almost endless. For example, the Rhema Bible Church in Tulsa, Oklahoma has a variety of recreational side-doors they call "L.I.N.K. Groups" ("Loving, Involving, Nurturing, Keeping"). Look at the names and descriptions of these groups, each one growing out of the passion of someone(s) in the church:

- ART (for creative and artful people)
- AVIATION (for licensed pilots to connect)
- OFF ROADING & CAMPING (family-friendly group with 4x4s)
- RHEMA RINGSIDE (boxing fans eat dinner and watch a good match on TV)
- ENTREPRENEUR (a network of entrepreneurs already in business ventures)
- HEALTH & WELLNESS (to study nutrition and attend health & wellness seminars)
- KNITTING, CROCHETING & QUILTING (for those who do or want to learn)
- MILITARY (those with military interests share stories and food together)
- GLORY RIDERS (rev up your motorcycles for joy rides and special events)
- SHARPS & FLATS (musicians, songwriters, singers develop their talents)
- PET LOVERS (enjoy speakers, pet care demonstrations, and volunteer)
- PHOTOGRAPHY (enjoy Phil Anglin's teaching masterful techniques)
- QUILTED GARDEN (green thumbs share gardening advice on flowers & veggies)
- QUILTING (work on projects and learn new techniques)
- RACQUETBALL (experienced and rookies enjoy matches and good times)
- ROADKILL HUNTING (go for game, share stories, learn the latest hunting techniques)
- SCRAPBOOK JUNKIES (enthusiasts have fun sharing their hobby together)

- SPOKESMAN BIKING (bicyclists meet for 5 – 10 mile rides together)
- SPORTSMAN FISHING (join in for fun and a relaxing good time)
- STAY-AT-HOME MOMS (domestic engineers enjoy laughter and food; child-care available)
- TIN CUP (golfing men gather to chase the little white ball)
- UBS: United Balloon Sculpturers (learn the fine art of balloon sculpture)
- WOMEN'S BOOK CLUB (ladies enjoy life-changing books together)
- WRITER'S BLOC (those with a passion for the written word develop their skills and enjoy writing opportunities)

In contrast, but just as strategic, Northridge Church in Plymouth, Michigan focuses more on side-doors that provide support through life's tougher times. They call their side-doors "LifeShare Groups." Here is their list of side-doors that are specifically for women. They have many others for men and families.

- BOUNDARIES (when to say "yes", and how to say "no"
- CHANGES THAT HEAL (for women who have been or are in unhealthy relationships)
- CHRONIC PAIN & ILLNESS ("why am I going through this?")
- OVERCOMING DEPRESSION & ANXIETY (Studies and discusses the book, *Learning to Tell Myself the Truth*)
- DIVORCE CARE (for hurting people experiencing the pain of separation)

- DOMESTIC ABUSE (there is HOPE through understanding the "root" of anger and abuse and uncover "Why Does He Do That?")
- FAMILY GROUP (for a family member or concerned friend of an alcoholic)
- FIRST PLACE (Transform Your Life with the Bible's Way to Weight Loss)
- GRIEFSHARE (to help those who are grieving physical death of a loved one)
- HOPEFUL HEARTS (a support group for couples or individuals dealing with infertility)
- 12 STEPS TO FREEDOM (for those who realize that alcohol or drugs are interfering with normal living)
- PARTNER CARE (learn how God loves addicted people differently and effectively)
- SHOUT! (a Christ-centered group for women in recovery from past physical and/or sexual abuse)
- LIVING BEYOND TRAUMA (for individuals and/or families who have experienced trauma through military duty, police or fire occupation, EMT and/or Medical personnel, victims of violent crime)

Side-doors mix people who share one or more things in common.

3. *Side-doors intentionally build relationships.*
Here's an important question about intended side-doors: "Are they places where people become real friends?" Effective side-doors are places where meaningful friendships don't just happen, they are planned. Side-doors are "relational greenhouses" where the seeds of friendships are planted, nurtured, watered...and grow. People in a side-door group play together, laugh together, cry together. As friendships grow, participants often spend time beyond the scheduled activities just sharing life together.

When people first begin attending a side-door activity they come because the topic is of interest to them. But an effective side-door leader will intentionally nurture relationships among group members. The graph below illustrates an interesting change in what members value in the group, and the reason for their continued participation:

Reasons for Attending

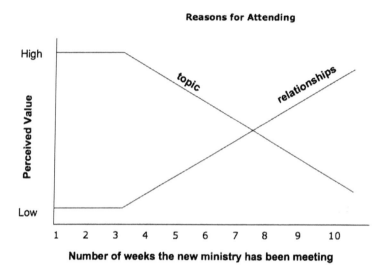

Number of weeks the new ministry has been meeting

In the first few weeks that people attend a new class, group, club, or activity, they are attracted by the opportunity to learn about a specific topic or participate in a specific experience. But as participants get to know each other and feel more and more comfortable together, the seeds of friendship are planted and begin to grow.

At some point, as the leader makes time for learning about, sharing with, and even praying for new friends, the value of the relationships actually becomes greater than the value of the content or activity. In fact, I have found that in about 75% of the groups, when they reach the end of their planned dissolution, they decide to continue meeting beyond that point. Why? Because they have come to value the relationship in and of themselves. The topic—the initial reason for their gathering—has become almost incidental. And that's good!

It is my experience that for this relational dynamic to occur, a side-door group or activity should meet *at least* six times over a six-month period. Of course, some side-door gatherings will meet weekly for years, and that's great. But a minimum of six meetings allows people to get to know each other, remember names, and start building history through common experiences. (More about how to build such community into your side-door gatherings later in this book.)

4. *Side-doors meet deeper human needs.*

One of the saddest things about a non-Christian's life is that they do not experience the joy, comfort, and peace that a relationship with God provides. While a side-door gathering need not be overtly spiritual, participants should get a taste of how God's love can speak to their deeper needs through the love of God's family. What are these deeper human needs that, when met, will give non-believers a first-hand taste of "glory divine"?

1. People feel disconnected and isolated. They are looking for a <u>place to belong</u> and feel part of a family or community.
2. People are feeling the pressure of a busy and stressful world. They are looking for a greater <u>sense of balance</u> and ways to manage priorities.
3. People sense the shallowness of superficial encounters with others. They are looking for <u>authentic relationships</u>.
4. People are feeling empty and drained from striving to meet their desires through work, material possessions, or entertainment. They are looking for <u>spiritual answers</u> to their unfulfilled "hunger."

5. People are feeling overwhelmed by the pace of change in every aspect of their world. They are looking for help through transitions.

When unchurched people can begin to feel a sense of hope that such needs can possibly be met in this church-related group, it provides a powerful attraction to the source of that hope. For example, suppose you are not a church attender but have been involved in a hiking group sponsored by a nearby church. Some months into the group, your wife needs to go into the hospital for surgery. The members of your hiking group bring food over for dinner. They pick up your 3rd grade son from school in the afternoon. They pray for your wife before their hikes and regularly ask about her condition. As she improves, they thank God for answered prayer. What effect do you think such caring acts will have on you, your wife, and your family?

In a word, I would call that "love." And the function of a healthy side-door group is to provide a place where people outside of the Christian faith can begin to experience God's love through God's people. When one or more of these deeper needs are met, Stanley Mooneyham's words ring true: "Love spoken can be easily turned aside. Love demonstrated is irresistible."[5] (Again, we'll learn how to see this happen later in the book.)

5. Side-doors require the involvement of a local church.

Architecturally speaking, a side-door must exist in some kind of a structure. You don't see side doors standing alone in the middle of a field. Spiritually speaking, the same principle applies. Side-doors cannot exist outside the ministry of a local church. They are not intended to simply do good works for needy people as an end in themselves. They are not designed to see people make a faith commitment, but never participate in a church. Side-doors connect people in a local church with people in a local community, with the goal of creating a relationship that brings them into the body of Christ. Believers who follow Christ are called to be a part of that Body, as arms, legs, hands, and feet. Side-door are built to reach lost people for Jesus Christ and add to the church daily those who are being saved (Acts. 2:47).

In this respect, I worry somewhat about the influence of the currently popular "missional movement" in how it moves people to value (or devalue) the local church. As an instructor at Wesley Seminary (Marion, IN), I teach a class called "The Missional Church." I have observed that many students, after reading books by missional authors and viewing videos of missional teachers, will throw the baby out with the bathwater. That is, they conclude that the ultimate goal of a "missional church" is to go into the community to do good works in the name of Christ and the expansion of "the Kingdom." And whether these needy folks ever come to faith and membership in a local church is not a great concern, and certainly not a criteria to define "success" in their missional agenda.

For example, a missionally inclined blogger recently lit into Andy Stanley's "5 million dollar bridge." North Point Community Church, a church known for its commitment to outreach and evangelism, has grown to the point where parking has become problematic. Stanley told his parishioners of the need to ease traffic congestion by constructing a bridge off of the main thoroughfare into the church. His letter included the following paragraph:

> Is it [the bridge] worth it? It all depends. If our mission is to be a church that's perfectly designed for the people who already attend, then we don't need a bridge. But if we want to continue to be a church unchurched people love to attend, then yes, it's worth it. From my perspective, this is not a "nice to have" option. Honestly, I don't want to raise money for, or

give money to, something that's not mission critical.
I believe creating a second access point allows us to
stay on mission. [6]

It seems obvious that Stanley's commitment, as pastor, is
to make disciples and assimilate them into the local church.
But the missional blogger responds:

This makes me sick. This is completely un-missional.
Missional churches are not attractional churches.
Missional churches send out their parishioners as
missionaries to the world, not bring them to church
over a five million dollar edifice set up to speed up
their exit and entry.[7]

In their zeal to create the Kingdom of God in the world,
some who "buy into" the missional movement seem to have
(or develop) a bias against the established church. Their
commitment is to "bring the Kingdom of God into the community." But the success of those kingdom-building efforts
does not seem to be evaluated on whether those who are
exposed to the Kingdom are ever reached and assimilated
into active membership and participation in a local church.

A commitment to side-doors, however, demands a "high
view" of the church—that the church is absolutely essential.
It is not *a* Body of Christ; it is *the* Body of Christ. Not just
a bride, but *the* bride of Christ. The Church is held to be the
central part of God's plan for the salvation and discipling
of people and nations. New converts must not only believe
in Jesus Christ, but must become responsible members of
the Church. If the Bible is to be taken seriously, we cannot
hold any other point of view. Becoming a Christian means
becoming a part of the Body. In fact, unless non-Christians
believe and become part of the Church, personified through
the local congregation, the ultimate value of our activities

must be questioned. This is the high view of the Church. A low view of the Church is that whether or not you belong to the Church is more or less a matter of choice. If you like it, you belong; if you don't, you don't.

Side-doors lead people into the Christian faith and community *through the local church*.

6. *Side-doors are managed and initiated by laypeople.*

A few years ago I was part of a study in which we asked pastors: "What is the most frustrating aspect of your ministry?" The number one response, regardless of denomination or theology, was: "Getting people in the church to participate in the work of the church."

The good news is that side-doors provide lay people with the opportunity to start and manage an activity in which they bring a personal interest and enthusiasm, and one which positively affects the life and growth of their church. Pastor's traditional problem—of motivating and involving people in ministry—ceases to be a problem, because the side-door activity taps into a passion which the member already has. In other words, they don't have to be motivated by a pastor... they are *already* motivated by a passion!

The bad news for some pastors, however, is that side-doors mean a loss of control. Rick Warren, whose church puts a strong emphasis on directing members' passions into ministries, has observed: "If you want your church to be a place where all sorts of talents and abilities are expressed in a creative way that draws people to Christ, you have to give up control and trust people with ministry."[8] A church that wants to start side-doors simply needs to identify the passions that are *already* in the congregation, and then channel them. In Chapter Four we will look at how to identify these passions that might become side-door ministries.

7. *Side-doors begin a disciple-making process.*

Most new Christians who become active church members have heard the Gospel more than once—from more than one source. In fact, one study found that those who became vital, growing Christians had heard the Gospel presented an average of 5.8 times before they made their commitment. This was in contrast to the number of times the Gospel was heard by those who made a decision but never became integrated into a church: on average, two![9] Multiple exposures to Christ through people and programs provide a more complete picture of what it means to be a Christ-follower.

The application? Side-door events should not be the only place an unchurched person encounters God. While a side-door activity will often be the first extended contact a unchurched person has with Christian people, it should not be the last. The new friends made in a side-door group/activity provide a natural context for invitations to other Christ-related events.

A non-member on your church softball team, for example, could be invited by a friend on the team to the church's Christmas Eve service, or special concert, or church beach trip. Inviting the friend's family to the church's Easter egg hunt or camping trip would be natural and appropriate. Even an invitation to attend a worship service may also be extended at some point, although it would probably be the fifth or sixth contact, rather than the second or third. The more Christian exposures a person has, the better they understand the implications of the Christian life and faith. In other words, side-doors are not isolated "entry events", but extended "entry paths" into the church.

8. *Side-doors make the benefit worth the cost.*

We all have places to go, people to see, things to do. That's life. But the choices we make about where we go, who we see, and what to do are based on our assessment of the benefits versus the cost. A side-door activity or group will prosper because participants tell their friends of its value. Therefore, in planning an effective side-door (which we will help you do in Part Two), the question must always be asked: "Will the benefit of participating be worth the cost?" The Prince of Peace Lutheran Church in Burnsville, Illinois has it right. When they consider starting a new side-door, they ask prospective attenders: "What kind of a group would you change your schedule to be a part of?"[10]

Suppose, for example, you are quite interested in developing a healthier lifestyle. With the encouragement of your church, you are excited by the prospect of beginning a women's fitness group. Would you find such an activity to be boring? Would you dread the meetings and count the seconds until its over? Of course not. You would love planning and participating in the group. You would meet new women who share your passion. You would make new friends. And what about those women in your group who don't attend your church but are committed to the goal of physical fitness? The health-related information they receive, the exercise they do, the encouragement they give and receive, the friends they make...those benefits far outweigh the costs.

The genius of side-door ministries, as you will discover in your own church, is that people enjoy being part of them. Members love them. Non-members love them. Because people love to do what they love to do...especially with others who love to do it, too. And the new relationships that develop around those passions become cherished.

chapter three

Does Your Church Need Side-Doors?

Would your church benefit from adding some (more) side-doors? Here are six self-diagnostic questions and measures to help you decide...

1. Do you have enough visitors to grow?

The answer to this question depends on your *Visitor Volume*. Visitor volume is the number of visitors/newcomers to your church-sponsored events, as a percentage of the total attendance. If you have a visitor volume of 5% or greater, you probably don't need any (more) side-doors. To calculate your Visitor Volume you will need to fill in the three columns in the chart below.

"Average Visitors" Column

- First, total the number of visitors/new contacts who attended one of your church-sponsored events in the past 52 weeks (including, but not limited to weekend services). Count 1st, 2nd, and 3rd time visitors (not just first-timers). Do not include visitors from out of town.
- Next, divide that total by the number of events from which you identified visitors (above). If you

counted visitors at events such as Maundy Thursday, Christmas Eve, etc., then include those events.

- This will give you the average number of visitors per event for the past year. Write this number in the upper left cell in the chart below under "Average Visitors" for the "Past 12 months". For a more reliable number, calculate your average number of visitors for the prior two years in the same way.

"Average Attendance" Column

- Total your attendance (including visitors) for the same events you used above for the past 52 weeks.
- Divide this total by the number of events, which will give you your average attendance per event. Calculate the previous two years for your "Average Attendance", as well.

"Visitor Volume" Column

- Divide your average number of visitors (first column) into your average attendance (second column). The result should be in the form of a percentage. If possible, complete the same calculation for the prior two years.

	Average Visitors	Average Attendance	Visitor Volume
Past 12 months			
13-24 months ago			
25-36 months ago			

Now, back to the question: "Do you have enough visitors to grow?" If your Visitor Volume is 5% or greater, you have enough visitors to grow. (Although, not every church with 5+% Visitor Volume grows, since there are other factors we will consider below.) If your Visitor Volume is significantly less than 5%, you need more side-doors, since the answer to the initial question is most likely, "No." There is a direct relationship between an increase in the number of newcomers involved in side-doors and the number of newcomers who visit your church service(s).

2. Do you keep enough visitors to grow?

The answer to this question depends on your *Visitor Retention*. Visitor Retention is the percentage of your visitors (from the left column in the chart above) who became involved in your church within a year of their first visit. They may not have yet joined as members, but they are now regularly attending one or more church activities. If you have a Visitor Retention of over 20% you probably do not need any (more) side-doors.

The best way to calculate your Visitor Retention is to list each person who has visited a church event in the past 2-18 months. Then determine whether that person is now a regular attender. An example of a chart for determining your Visitor Retention is given below, although it would need to be much longer, allowing for each visitor's name to be listed on a row.

Once you have completed this chart, simply add the number of YESes in the right column, and divide that number into the total number of visitors on the chart. The result will be your Visitor Retention.

Name of Visitor	Date of first visit (in past 2 – 18 months)	Now regularly attending? (YES/NO)
(continued)		

A healthy Visitor Retention rate is 20%. That is, if you are keeping 1 out of 5 visitors, you are doing very well. If your Visitor Retention is less than 20% you should consider adding additional side-doors. Individuals who visit your church who are already involved in a side-door group have a much higher retention rate than walk-in visitors.

3. How many of your present activities are side-doors?

To answer this question, copy the chart below onto a separate page and add enough rows to list every church-sponsored activity that meets at least monthly.

In the first column list the activity. This includes youth events, children and adult classes, small groups, support groups, choir, sports teams, etc. Do not include your worship services, since those are "front doors". Also, do not include church board or committee meetings. Finally, do not include activities sponsored by organizations that use your facilities but are not sponsored by your church.

In the second column, calculate the average attendance for each meeting during the past six months. (Total the number from each meeting, then divide by the number of meetings.)

In the third column, record the average number of unchurched people in these meeting. (Add the total number of *unchurched* people at each meeting, then divide by the number of meetings.)

In the fourth column calculate the percentage of unchurched people in each activity. (Divide the third column into the second column.)

In the fifth column, determine which groups are functioning as side-doors. If column 4 is between 25% - 75%, the answer is: "Yes." If it is less than 25%, or over 75%, write in "No".

Finally, calculate the TOTALS (at the bottom of the chart).

Church groups/activities (meet at least monthly)	Avg. attendance (past 6 months)	Average # of unchurched in attendance	% of unchurched	"Side-door"? (YES/ NO)
(continued)				
TOTAL #:				

The rule of thumb is that at least 20% of your existing church activities (classes, small groups, monthly socials, youth gatherings, men's & women's groups, etc.) should be side-doors. If your number is lower, consider adding new side-doors.

4. *How many of your new members/attenders were unchurched?*

People come into a church through one of three ways:

"Biological"— Children of exiting Christians becoming part of the church.

"Transfer"— Existing Christians transferring from a previous church.

"Conversion"— People committing or re-dedicating their life to Christ and connecting with the church.

I have noticed that what often appears to be significant growth in a church turns out to be primarily transfer growth, or just a case of congregational "musical chairs". Conversion growth, of course, is what Christ was talking about when he said, "...go and make disciples." Healthy churches see at least 20% of their newcomers who are both new to that local church, and also to Christ's church (i.e., conversion).

Complete the chart below to help you consider the source of your newcomers. If possible, include information for the past five years.

	Conversion		Transfer		Biological		TOTAL	
	#	%	#	%	#	%	#	%
5 years ago								100%
4 years ago								100%
3 years ago								100%
2 years ago								100%
Last year								100%
TOTAL								100%

If your average conversion growth rate over the past five years is less than 20% of your total growth, I suggest that you need more side-doors. If your rate is between 20% - 40%, you are healthy. If it is over 40%, and your church is over ten years old, write a book! (Most new churches typically have a conversion rate over 50%, but within ten years the percentage will most likely have declined.) Regardless of your conversion rate, if you regularly start side-doors, you will increase the number of unchurched people with whom you come in contact, and the number of those who will move from outside of Christ's family and your church to inside.

5. *What is your church's approach to lay ministry?*

Churches will typically utilize their members through one of two different approaches. There may not have been an intentional choice made. But every church is clearly in one camp or the other: The *Institutional* approach, or the *Individual* approach.

An Institutional approach to lay ministry begins with the needs of the church institution. Every church needs Sunday School teachers, committee members, musicians. There are just certain personnel needs that a church will have if it is to conduct effective ministry. In the Institutional approach, when a role or task position opens up in a church, the response is to search for a person who seems most suitable to fill the job. "Success," in such churches, is when a member says, "OK. I'll take the job." Hopefully the person is qualified, gifted, and motivated for that area of ministry; but there are no guarantees. If it turns out to be a mismatch between member and task, the predictable result is a poorly done task and a frustrated member. "Plugging warm bodies into ministry slots in a congregation," says Pam Heaton, "tends to increase volunteer burnout, dissatisfaction, and departure."[1] With the Institutional approach to lay ministry, church members exist to serve the needs of the institution.

The *Individual* approach is far less widely practiced, but tends to be much more effective in terms of significant lay mobilization. Here the priority of lay ministry is not so much to fill a vacancy, but to identify a place where church members (and even non-members) can find fulfillment and personal growth that compliment their interests and abilities. Rather than beginning with the needs of the institution, the Individual approach begins with the strengths of the person. Church members are encouraged to try a position related to their interest and see how it "fits." If it does, the member may chose to spend more time in that ministry and/or receive training. If the task is not comfortable, or the person does not feel a sense of calling, he/she is encouraged to explore other ministries that might be a better fit. If a natural match cannot be found between existing roles and church member, the possibility of creating a new ministry is explored. In the Individual approach to lay ministry the institution exists for the benefit of the people rather than the people for the benefit of the institution.

Consider this matrix that describes the typical results of these two approaches to lay ministry:

Ministry Measure	Institutional Approach	Individual Approach
Percent of the church community involved in ministry	Less than 20%	More than 20%
Individual's satisfaction with ministry task	Often frustrated	Usually fulfilled
Personal energy level as a result of the task	Drained	Rejuvenated
Reason for participating	Doing what I must	Doing what I like
Effect on interpersonal church relationships	Friction	Fusion
Number of people declining to serve	Many	Few
Resignations from the task throughout the year	Frequent	Infrequent
Church leaders' motivation for filling the role	Institutional need	Individual growth
Frequency of new ministries created	Seldom	Often

A church's philosophy of lay ministry, like many things in life, is not always simple to determine. And, rather than being entirely an "either-or" situation, it more likely falls somewhere on the following continuum:

PHILOSOPHY OF LAY MINISTRY

←——————————————————————————————→

Institutional   *Individual*

Church leaders who wish to create a "greenhouse" for effective lay ministry must consciously keep pushing the church toward the right side of this scale, because the "gravitational pull" of institutional demands is always to the left. "One of the key challenges facing a pastor is to position the church as a creative place that needs the expression of all sorts of talents and abilities; not just singers, ushers, and Sunday School teachers," says Rick Warren. "One of the reasons enthusiasm is so low in many churches is that creativity is discouraged.[2]

6. *What percentage of your members are ministers?*

The chart below will help you discern whether your church's philosophy of lay ministry either facilitates or frustrates the creation of new side-doors. To assess your church, first fill in the blank at the top left on line 1—your "TOTAL CHURCH CONSTITUENCY". (I know. It reminds me of a tax form, too.) This number reflects your overall church family (that is, a combination of church members and regular attenders). Next, determine in which column your church falls on lines 2-18. All the numbers are percentages. Calculate your percentages based on your "total church constituency" (line 1), unless otherwise noted.

If you find your scores fall primarily in the left columns, the focus of your lay ministry is likely to be inward and your people are "workers." The farther your scores are to the right, the more likely you have an outward focus and your people are "ministers." It is on the right side, obviously, where effective lay ministry most often occurs. Such ministry is about growing people in Christ, not filling slots to accomplish our institutional needs.

"Workers" ⟷ "Ministers"

	1. TOTAL CHURCH CONSTITUENCY: _____	PROBLEM AREA	NEEDS ATTENTION	AVERAGE	GOOD	IDEAL
People Involved	2. Constituents with a specific role/task	0-20	21-29	30-49	50-69	70+
	3. Constituents with a "church-focused" role (% of #2)	96+	95-86	85-75	74-61	60>
	4. Constituents with an "outward-focused" role (% of #2)	0-4	5-9	10-14	15-19	20+
	5. Constituents who attended worship 1+ in past 4 months	0-34	35-44	45-59	60-69	70+
	6. Total # of constituents involved in a small group	0-10	11-29	30-45	46-64	65+
New Attenders	7. Constituents who began attending in last 12 months	0-2	3-4	5-6	7-10	11+
	8. New constituents (from #7) with a role/task	0-29	30-44	45-59	60-69	70+
	9. New constituents (from #7) involved in a small group	0-29	30-49	50-69	70-79	80+
	10. Constituents who began attending 12-24 months ago	0-2	3-4	5-6	7-10	11+
	11. Constituents (from #10) with a role/task	0-29	30-44	45-59	60-69	70+
	12. Constituents (from #10) involved in a small group	0-29	30-49	50-69	70-79	80+
Ministry Positions	13. Total role/task positions available in the church	0-20	21-29	30-49	50-69	70+
	14. Role/task positions with written job description	0-10	11-29	30-50	51-74	75+
	15. Positions with specific pre-service training	0-10	11-29	30-50	51-69	70+
	16. "Maintenance" oriented role/task positions (from #13)	90+	89-80	79-70	69-60	59>
	17. "Outreach" oriented role/task positions (from #13)	0-8	9-15	16-20	21-34	35+
	18. New roles/tasks created in the last 12 mo. (from #13)	0-2	3-4	5-6	7-10	11+

Source: *The Growth Report* Vol. 2 No. 6, Institute for American Church Growth (Pasadena, CA)

The Next Step

The chances are good, having worked through the diagnostic exercises in this chapter, that your church would benefit from some (more) side-doors. There is really only one "downside" to the prospect of more people starting more creative ministries in your church. It is that a commitment to equipping and encouraging your saints for the work of ministry won't happen by itself. It takes a priority among the leadership of the church. Left to natural patterns, you will find that, at best, 20% of the members will be doing 80% of the tasks. And of the tasks being done, 95% will be inward-focused. This is obviously not a formula for successful lay ministry. And sometimes it can get a little messy when you're dealing with people in the world who haven't yet been "cleaned up".

But ministry is what the church is called to do. Ministry is what Jesus came to do: "I have come not to be ministered to, but to minister" (Matt. 20:28). And the more ministry we do, the more likely we will be rewarded with the Master's words: "Well done thou good and faithful servant."

So, now let's look at *how* to encourage and involve people throughout your church to build side-doors. Not only is it one of the most effective ways to reach new people. It's easier than you ever imagined possible. And, to beat it all... it's fun! ☺

chapter four

"Heartbeat Ministry" —Side-Doors From Your Church Member's Perspective

Let's talk for a moment about quarters—25¢ pieces. If you look at one in your pocket you'll see a likeness of the father of our country. But turn it over and, if you happen to have one of the state collection quarters, you'll find an interesting montage of images representing a particular state. And, if you have several such quarters in your pocket, chances are good that you will see different images on each one.

George Washington is on the Maryland quarter, he's on the Oregon quarter. He's on Montana, Illinois, and Texas. They are all quarters. And they all look the same...on one side. But on the other side, they are different. Each quarter is unique, fascinating, and reflects the particular identity of one of our states.

The similarity, yet variety, in the state quarters helps me to understand a relationship between two terms we will be using throughout the rest of this book. One term you are now familiar with—"Side-doors." The new, but very related term I would like to introduce to you is—"Heartbeat Ministry."

Up to this point we have been looking at the "George Washington" half; namely, side-doors. Side-doors are a strategy that will help any local church reach out to and connect with people in their community. Big churches can have side-doors; little churches can all have side-doors. Urban, rural, growing, declining churches can have side-doors. Any church that desires to be more missional and more effective in ministry will find side-doors a great asset. Like the George Washington side of the state quarter, side-doors are a constant and consistent strategy that just works.

"Heartbeat Ministry" is the other side of the quarter. It is how church members will see the process of side-doors—from their unique, personal, individual perspective. The variety of unique Heartbeat Ministries that people can start will take many different appearances. Motorcycles may be a passion for several young men in the church. Developing a Heartbeat ministry around their particular interest could become an effective side-door to build relationships with non-members. A support group for adults with ADHD might become a much different kind of Heartbeat ministry for several others, and another side-door for your church. A quilting club could be the passion—or heartbeat—of several older women in your church, while a divorced dad's Heartbeat ministry may be born out of the experience of others. All these will be quite different on one hand. But they will all have the similarity of being side-doors into your church.

In analyzing the characteristics of growing, "apostolic" churches, researcher George Hunter observes that the leaders of those churches take seriously the potential of side-doors and, as a result, "...one finds churches reaching deaf people, and gambling addicts, and single parent families, and people with mental illnesses, and Laotian immigrants—because a team of people within the church began following their hearts."[1]

Any passion of a church member(s) has the potential of developing into a Heartbeat ministry for that person, and a side-door for your church. Heartbeat ministries grow out of the unique interests found among the people of your church. And each Heartbeat ministry will look different because each is started by different people with different passions—different heartbeats. So, in this chapter, and throughout this book, I hope to add the term "Heartbeat Ministry" to your vocabulary.

Introducing Heartbeat Ministry...

It is not difficult to understand the idea of side-doors in a church. Hopefully you have a pretty good fix on that already. But actually seeing people in your church successfully nurture their passions into healthy, contagious side-doors—Heartbeat Ministries—is not as easy. Most have never done anything quite like starting a new ministry. The intimidation factor, alone, can be enough to snuff out the spark.

To help guide church members who have the passion but not the experience of starting a new ministry, I developed a planning guide called, How to Start a Heartbeat Ministry. This workbook is written specifically for those people with the dream of starting a new ministry. To introduce you to what a Heartbeat Ministry is, I have   reproduced the Introduction and Chapter One from this guidebook below. It is what a "Ministry Planning Team" in a church would first read as they begin planning to start a new ministry around their particular passion. I hope it will also help you to better see the potential of enthusiastic men and women in your church pursuing their heartbeat in Christ-honoring, people focused ministry.

INTRODUCTION

Twenty thousand feet above the earth moisture begins to concentrate. Molecules of hydrogen and oxygen condense. Small droplets of water materialize and begin falling to earth.

At the outset of their journey the little raindrops all look about the same. They are spheres of water 2 mm in diameter with a similar composition and density. But as they encounter frigid air currents blowing up and down, back and forth, the droplets condense around microscopic dust particles in the atmosphere. And a marvelous transformation begins to occur. The little raindrops start turning into...snowflakes. They change at different times, speeds, and altitudes. But by the time each gently settles to earth, not one snowflake is the same as another. Their journey has transformed them.

Our lives are similar to those snowflakes. At the outset of our journey we all look about the same: tiny embryos only a few centimeters in diameter with the same composition and density. But then, at birth, we begin our unique journey. We encounter certain events...meet certain people...develop certain attitudes. We experience joy... pain... love... apathy. Our journey transforms us.

All of your life experiences to this point, have shaped you. Some more than others. Perhaps you lost a parent in early childhood, or a child in early parenthood. Maybe you survived cancer, or are fighting to. Maybe it was abuse or divorce that highly influenced the snowflake you are today.

Or, in your youth you may have been quite physically coordinated and developed a passion for sports as a hobby or profession. Do you have a love for camping because of good times with family and friends? Possibly an experience in your background sparks deep compassion for unwed teenage mothers...or widows who have lost a lifetime mate...or the joy of riding a motorcycle on a summer cross-country tour. Whatever the experiences, whatever the influences...your "snowflake" is unique.

But, so what?

The answer to that question is both simple, yet profound: *God doesn't waste experience!*

Whoever you are, and whatever you have been becoming, the uniqueness that is you can be used by God. The special person you now are might be used in a way that only you and God can imagine. Maybe, at this point, even you can't. But Scripture tells us, "...all things work together for good to those who love God, to those who are called according to His purpose" (Romans 8:28). In this verse God is not just talking about you. He is talking to you: "I will work your life experiences together in a powerful way if you love me and let me use the unique person that you have become."

Purpose of This Workbook

This book is a guide to help you tap into your unique "snowflake"...for divine purposes. It is an exciting process. And a very enjoyable one. Just ask the tens of thousands of Christian men and women in churches around the country today who are using their uniqueness in Christ-honoring ministry. I know because I've talked to many of them. I've seen their eyes light up when they tell their stories. I've watched their body language saying, "this is just *SO* cool!" (Or words to that effect, depending on their particular generation.)

Job Networking Ministry
Johns Creek United Methodist
Church (Duluth, GA)
The Career Network meets the 2nd and 4th Wednesday of each month at 7p.m. Twenty to thirty people (members and non members) typically attend each meeting.

This workbook is a guide to help you focus the special power of your uniqueness...into a new ministry. Like a magnifying glass that focuses the sun's dispersed light into a powerful and penetrating beam of heat, this workbook will help you focus the uniqueness of who you are into a powerful and productive new ministry in your church.

We'll discuss the term "ministry" in the first chapter. But, basically, its just a place where people are touched by God's love. And when you're in the middle of it all, that really is *SO* cool!!

You have had a life full of experiences; some pleasant, some not. And those experiences have shaped you into a unique person that God can use to love others. But here's the most exciting part: Many of those "others" that God wants to love are people living in your neighborhood right now—who are outside of a Christian faith and community. They don't know it, but some will come to be Christ-followers in the months and years ahead…because of the ministry you will have helped to birth.

But God does not demand that we use our experience in ministry. His modus operandi is that He *invites*…but He does not *force*.

Golf Club
Bethel Church (San Jose, CA)
The Bethel Church Golf Club is open to men, women, and children interested in the game of golf. Tournaments are scheduled throughout the year.

So, the next step is up to you. Are you ready to explore the possibility that God has been preparing you for something special and unique? Something that will positively change your life, and the lives of some people you do not even yet know? I hope so, because… HEY! Hold on a minute… Look up in the sky. Can you believe that?!

It's starting to *snow!!!*

CHAPTER ONE
So, You Want To Start Something?

You have something on your mind. Everyone does. What's on your mind is what's important to you. It's what you think about. What you look forward to. What you worry about. How you spend your free time.

Women's Prison Ministry
Grace Church (Eden Prairie, MN)
A team of 7-10 women from Grace Church go to the Shakopee Prison on the second Sunday morning of each month to conduct worship services for 50-60 women.

What is it for you? A hobby? Perhaps you're passionate about fishing... or quilting...or reading...or photography.

Maybe your heart beats for a cause. Do you find fulfillment in helping with the needs of the homeless...or children in single parent families... or people struggling with addictions?

Perhaps you're not actually *doing* anything at the moment about your particular interest. Maybe you just *wish* you could...or think that someone should.

Everyone cares about something. In fact, most people get passionate about a number of things. Some care so much that they do something about it. Some through their church!

That's what this workbook is all about. It's a guide to walk you through the process of turning your "heartbeat" into a heartbeat ministry in your church.

What is a "Heartbeat Ministry"?

Starting heartbeat ministries is an increasingly popular and effective way for people and churches to reach into their community and touch others with God's love. A heartbeat ministry blossoms out of the passion of one or more church members who care about something (anything, really) and are open to letting God do something with that passion.

We will use the term "ministry" quite often in this workbook (i.e., "starting a new ministry"). But always remember that the term is very flexible. For example, a heartbeat ministry in the Brethren in Christ Church (Alta Loma, CA) is a regular support group for recovering alcoholics, started by a member of the church. A heartbeat ministry in the Bethel AME Church (Wilmington, DE) is the "Daisy Jackson Homework Club" that meets twice a week and grew out of the passion of...can you guess?! Or, a heartbeat ministry in the Thomas Road Baptist Church (Lynchburg, VA) is a group of guys who get together Sunday mornings for Bible study and then go for a motorcycle ride after church.

A heartbeat ministry is simply a means by which a church encourages individual members to create a ministry and bring people together around a shared interest. And, when people connect around one or more heartfelt passions, a wonderful thing happens. New friends are made. A sense of community develops.

And one of the most beautiful things in God's creation begins to flourish—relationships.

While heartbeat ministries can take hundreds of different forms, there is one common ingredient they all share. All heartbeat ministries involve both Christians and non-Christians. This is no "holy huddle" for believers only. A heartbeat ministry brings together members and non-members around a common interest or concern which they all share. And through their common passion, relationships develop that breakdown barriers which have often isolated people inside the church from people outside.

Throughout the pages of this workbook I have included "peepholes" into various heartbeat ministries in churches around the country, along with a brief description from their website. For example, in this workbook is a peephole into a heartbeat ministry at Grace United Methodist Church in Florida. Begun by several members who enjoyed puppets and wanted to turn their interest outward, the Puppet Ministry of Grace Church has become a great vehicle to build friendships among members and non-members who have an interest in puppets. Take a moment, if you haven't already done so, to flip through the pages of this workbook and look at just a few heartbeat ministries in churches around the country...

And these are just a handful of great ministries that grew from a heartbeat. A heartbeat ministry begins with an interest or concern of someone(s) in the church. These people are then encouraged and guided to turn their interest outward...into a ministry. It's a win... win...win situation. Church members win because they're doing something they already enjoy and are probably good at. Churches win because they are broadening their ministry and connections with people outside the church. And people who become involved in these ministries win because their lives are positively touched by God and God's people.

My Assumptions About You

Because you are reading this workbook, I assume that...

You are a Christian. You have a relationship with God through His Son, Jesus Christ. And a great deal of the meaning and purpose in your life is built on this foundation.

You are involved in a church. You may not be a "big shot" in your church. In fact, for the purpose of this workbook, it's probably better if you're not. But you do have a church you call "home."

Overeaters Anonymous
Holladay Church of Christ
(Holladay, UT)
Through a twelve-step program, Overeaters Anonymous helps compulsive overeaters recover physically, emotionally, and spiritually.

You believe that Christians (including you) should be a "channel" for God's love to flow to those around them. It's true. People experience God's love through the love of God's people. And such love experienced attracts non-Christians to the source.

You have priorities. There are some things that are important to you. And you are open to letting God use at least one of those somethings to connect with others who care about the same thing.

If you meet all these criteria...keep reading. There are some exciting times ahead for you and your church.

The above pages are taken from the Introduction and Chapter One in the workbook *How to Start a Heartbeat Ministry.* The entire workbook is available as a stand-alone resource for members' who are planning a Heartbeat ministry. Copies of *How to Start a Heartbeat Ministry* may be purchased at: www.Heartbeatministries.net, or by calling: 800-844-9286.

So, that's the idea of Heartbeat Ministries...the best way to build side-doors into your church. They provide a creative opportunity for people in your church to connect with people in your community—around common interests. As new friendships develop around those common interests, new entry paths open up for outsiders to become insiders in God's family and your church.

But there is an important question to answer before we see Heartbeat ministries sprouting up in your church. Perhaps it is already on your mind. Your question should be: "How do we find the people in our church who have the passion, the motivation, and the desire to begin a Heartbeat ministry?" In the next chapter we're going to get practical about finding the passion that may spark a new ministry in your church. Then we will go through the step-by-step process of starting a Heartbeat ministry that will fan the spark into a roaring flame!

Part Two

How to Start
a Heartbeat Ministry

chapter five

Find the Passion

What an insight into God's creativity to observe how different we are from each other. Not only physically, but psychologically, intellectually, emotionally. Our cognitive maps are as different as our fingerprints. We are interested in different things...enthusiastic about different topics...passionate about different causes. Everyone is interested in something. But those "somethings" are as vast as the landscape of our mind.

Motivational experts know that the best way to energize people is to tap into something they already care about. It's the same in the church. An effective lay ministry process matches people's unique interests, enthusiasms, and passions with tasks that compliment those unique interests, enthusiasms, and passions. Here's a simple but powerful secret to seeing people enthusiastically involved in ministry:

Channel enthusiasm; don't try to change it!

Low member involvement and/or satisfaction in a church is a symptom, not a problem. The problem may be that there are not enough places for people to get involved. The situation would like this:

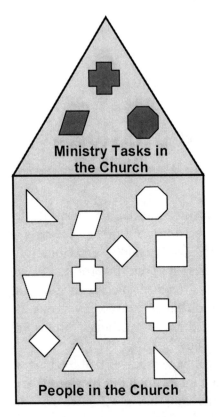

The diagram illustrates that there are not enough ministry roles for the number of people in the church. Research indicates that an ideal role-to-member ratio is 60:100. That is, in a healthy church there will be approximately 60 places of ministry/service for every 100 people. An unhealthy ratio is closer to 27:100.[1]

Another possible cause of low member involvement and/or satisfaction is that there aren't enough "right" places for people to get involved. The situation would look like this:

Ministry Tasks in
the Church

People in the Church

Here the roles to member ratio is adequate, but members are square pegs trying to fit into round holes. Or, to be more accurate, square pegs, trapezoid pegs, triangle pegs, octagon pegs and many other sized pegs trying to fit into round holes. There just aren't enough of the right shaped holes to go around.

This book will help you in both cases. It will help you increase the *number* of ministry positions, as well as the *variety* of ministry opportunities that exist in your church. It's about how to successfully cut the right shaped holes for the "pegs" God has put in your church.

How to Find the Passion

Everyone in your church, unless they are in a coma, cares about something. Most people care about a lot of things. They have particular interests…various concerns…intense passions. Successful side-doors are birthed out of people's priorities. If you can tap into the passions of the members in your church you will be like Uncle Jed who missed the rabbit, but hit something far more valuable: "…up from the ground come bubblin' crude." Hit passion in your church and you will have struck black gold! (If you were born after 1971, ask your parents about Uncle Jed.)

First, develop an ongoing way to listen for passion in your church. "Start where your people are," says the pastor of First Baptist Church in Leesburg, Florida, a church that has transitioned from an institutional to incarnational approach to lay ministry. "Find the need that most touches their hearts and they will give themselves to it. Even people who are not directly affected by a problem may feel deeply about it."[2] You're like the guy at the park with the metal detector and headphones who walks back and forth listening for anything that goes "ping." Put on your headphones, start walking around, and listen for passion.

My friend, Ricardo Zapata, pastor of Principe De Paz Iglesia de los Brethren in Santa Ana, California, recently told me that he had noticed many of the boys and men in his church going to the local park before church to play soccer. In fact, sometimes when the game was tied, they would be late for church. "One day it dawned on me," he said. "If you can't beat them, join them." He asked several of the men if they would help organize a church soccer league. It took off like wild fire.

Here are some ways to identify passion in the people God has put in your church.

1. What you already know. If you've been at the church for any length of time, you already know something about the lives of those in your church. Try this exercise. Take ten 4x6 cards. Put the name of one person in your church at the top of each card. Then, below each name, jot down any issues, observations, or concerns you are aware of that are important to each person (i.e., family situation, health concern, significant life experiences, special interest, etc.). Then look over these cards. There should be clues of possible Heartbeat ministries based just on what you already know about people.

A useful way to keep such information is a computer program. Develop (or purchase) a system that lets you keep information on the passions, interests, concerns, and significant life experiences of people. More sophisticated church software programs have coding and search capabilities so you can later get a report of all the people in your database who share a common interest or concern. This can obviously be helpful later in bringing like-minded people together.

2. Life Transitions. One of the constants in life is change. Some change is chosen (like marriage, relocation, having children). Other change just happens (like aging, losing a job, having children). Life happens. And not all of the things that happen in life feel that great. But one of my favorite life-lines is: *"God doesn't waste experience!"* Many Heartbeat ministries have grown out of pretty tough experiences. Strokes. Car accidents. Disabled children. Chronic pain.

Below is an interesting and potentially very helpful tool. It's called the "Social Readjustment Scale."[3] In layman's language, it's a stress scale. It identifies the "bumps" in life. Maybe you've seen this before. It originally came from research by two cardiologists at the University of Washington Medical School who were studying the risk of heart attacks. The numbers on the right indicate the relative stress of each life event on a scale from 1 - 100.

Life Event	Rank
1. Death of a spouse	100
2. Divorce	73
3. Marital separation	65
4. Jail term	63
5. Death of a close family member	63
6. Personal injury or illness	53
7. Marriage	50
8. Fired from work	47
9. Marital reconciliation	45
10. Retirement	45
11. Change in health of family member	44
12. Pregnancy	40
13. Sex difficulties	39
14. Gain a new family member	39
15. Business readjustment	39
16. Change in financial state	38
17. Death of a close friend	37
18. Change to different line of work	36
19. Change in number of arguments with spouse	35
20. Mortgage over $300,000	31
21. Foreclosure of mortgage or loan	30
22. Change in responsibilities at work	29
23. Son or daughter leaving home	29
24. Trouble with in-laws	29
25. Outstanding personal achievement	28
26. Spouse begins or stops work	26
27. Begin or end school	26
28. Major change in living conditions	25
29. Change in work/sleep habits.	24
30. Trouble with boss	23
31. Change in work hours or conditions	20
32. Change in residence	20
33. Change in schools	20
34. Change in recreational pursuit	19
35. Change in church activities	19
36. Change in social activities	18
37. Mortgage or loan less than $300,000	17
38. Change in sleeping habits	15
39. Change in number of family get-togethers	15
40. Change in eating habits	15

As you look at this list, do you see any events that someone in your church has lived through in the last five years? If so, think about the possibility of a Heartbeat ministry in your church developed by people who have "been there and done that."

I shared this scale at a seminar a few years ago in Ventura, California. At the break a man in his mid-40s came up to me and said, "You know, there's something missing on this scale that's even higher than losing your spouse."

I thought he might be joking, but his face did not show it. "What's that?" I asked.

"The death of a child," he responded as his eyes teared up. He had lost his teenage son to suicide six months earlier. But he went on to tell me that he was in the process of working with his church to develop a ministry to families who had also lost a child. "Parents are supposed to go *before* their kids, not after," he said. "It's tough going through something like that. But when you can talk with someone who knows how you feel, it makes a big difference. So, that's what I'm trying to do through our church." Now there was a Heartbeat ministry if ever I heard one! God doesn't waste experience.

When people in your church hit life's bumps, they need support. That's one of the wonderful things about being part of Christ's body. Yet a big part of the healing, or coping with those bumps can be in helping others—in or outside the church—over the same bumps. Actually, the process has been going on for years: "God comes along side us when we go through hard times," wrote the Apostle Paul. "And before you know it, he brings us alongside someone else who is going through hard times so that we can be there for that person, just as God was there for us" (II Cor. 1:4). God doesn't waste experience.

3. Conversations. Casual comments, hallway chats, an exchange after church. It's surprising how many clues can be picked up in simple conversations ... when you're listening for passion. Enthusiasm is better discovered from casual conversations than by commissioned research. "How many years will it take a committee to decide what affinity groups we want to target?" wonders a responder to a pastoral blog.[4]

I remember being driven to the Louisville airport by a woman staff member of a church where I had just finished consulting. I tried a few topics of conversation, but nothing seemed to catch. Her responses were short and she made no effort to nurture the conversation. Then I mentioned something about my teenage son who has ADHD, and the challenge it was just to get him through a night of homework. She lit up. Her 13-year old daughter had a similar learning disability. She was frustrated with the school district and thinking about pulling her child out to do home schooling. But she was divorced and could not afford to be without an income. Wow! Had I touched a nerve! She couldn't stop talking about all the choices she was facing, and how she wished she could talk with someone who did home schooling, or who knew about options she had with the school district. I wondered how many other mom's in the church and community might be in similar situations, and how a topic of so much passion might be a great Heartbeat ministry. Everyone is passionate about something! It's just a matter of finding the "hot button."

Not every passion needs to grow into a Heartbeat ministry. But every Heartbeat ministry needs to grow out of passion. When you and other church leaders are thinking Heartbeat ministries, conversations are like prospecting for gold—listening, engaging, exchanging opinions that could lead to a "mother lode" of passion.

4. New Members Orientation. Most pastors feel that it is desirable to see new members involved in ministry early in their membership. I agree. The new member class is a great time to help people match their passion and gifts with the right ministry. It's also a great time to consider starting a new ministry if an existing match is not obviously forthcoming. Of course, with new members, you'll want to consider how well you know the person, their spiritual maturity, and their previous experience. But don't try to force new member "pegs" into existing ministry "holes" if they don't fit.

5. *You Are Special!* booklet.[5] This 24-page color booklet is an excellent way to spread the word that your church is in the ministry mid-wife business. The booklet tells the story of common people who 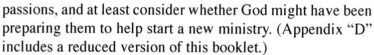 discovered a way to turn their interest outward into a ministry through their church. Readers are encouraged to think about their own interests, concerns, and passions, and at least consider whether God might have been preparing them to help start a new ministry. (Appendix "D" includes a reduced version of this booklet.)

6. *Pastoral Counseling.* A pastor friend in Temple City, California recently told me about a developing Heartbeat ministry in their church where the idea was birthed out of a counseling session. A young couple came in to talk to the pastor about their 14-year old son who had been caught shop-lifting for the first time. The parents, of course, were distraught.

The pastor knew that another family in the church also had a teenage son who had had several run-ins with local law enforcement. The pastor asked if he could introduce the young couple to the other parents. The two couples, of course, had much in common and became close friends. With the pastor's encouragement, they began talking about how a support group, or some kind of ministry through the church, might be started for families in similar situations.

About three months after the couples started talking about such a ministry—and long before any actual program had been developed—the church began receiving phone calls from people in the community asking about the program for parents with troubled teens. Somehow, apparently through just some casual comments, the rumor had gotten out that this church had a support group for families with teenagers having problems. They were getting calls before a program had even been developed, let alone publicized! The secret to success is to find a need and fill it.

Of course, not every pastoral counseling session will generate a Heartbeat ministry. But when pastors and lay counselors develop "side-door sensitivity," this can be another source for turning problems into possibilities. Remember, God doesn't waste experience!

7. *"I Wish" cards.* I got this idea from Lyle Schaller years ago at a workshop he was leading. Simply print some 4x6 cards similar to the one below and place them in various locations around the church (pew racks, information center, etc.).

I WISH...

"When I think of our church and ways we could make a difference in the lives of people in this community, I WISH we could have a ministry for:

_____

_____

_____

_____

If you would be interested in helping to see this wish come true, write your name and contact information below. (Chances improve immensely that something will actually happen if you're willing to be a part.) Then, put this card in the offering or give it to an usher. We look forward to hearing from you! Thanks.

Name (optional): _____

Phone: _____ e-mail: _____

Mention these cards periodically in the worship service announcements and the church newsletter. Review them and respond.

8. *Congregational Survey.* You can gather information fairly efficiently through a congregational survey. A good survey will identify interests, concerns, and passions in your church. You can then categorize the responses into common groups. Examining these groupings will spark some creative ideas about possible side-door ministries. For example, you may learn that six people in your church have grandchildren living in their home. While none of the grandparents may approach you with the idea of a ministry to people in this situation (or even have thought about it), you could identify possible interest through a brief exploratory meeting after church one Sunday for anyone with grandchildren living at home. Collecting and then analyzing a congregational survey is a good way to "prime the pump" for possible Heartbeat ministries.

Appendix A provides a sample survey you are welcome to use or adapt. It is also available to download at www. HeartbeatMinistries.net. Notice that the "Stress Scale" we looked at earlier is the last item on the survey. I hope you're thinking what I'm thinking…

9. *Sermons.* One or a series of sermons can help create a culture where people with passions are encouraged to consider whether God could use them in starting a new ministry. A sermon about how every Christian is called to be Christ-like (incarnational evangelism, remember)…to serve rather than be served…to use their experiences for ministry…and how God doesn't waste experience are all great themes quite complimentary to the idea of Heartbeat ministry.

A sermon can also sensitize listeners to events in their lives in which God may be nudging them in a new ministry direction. For example, a month ago (as of this writing) Jason, a high school kid in Aumsville, Oregon showed up at the Mountain View Wesleyan Church asking to do community service hours. He only needed a day or two to fulfill his commitment. The pastor enlisted Shelby, an older adult member and the resident handyman, to work with Jason doing small projects around the church. The outcome was that Jason worked longer than he needed, came to church the next Sunday to sit with Shelby, and brought his brother the following week. This experience stirred in Shelby a previously latent desire to mentor young people, and he is currently exploring a new ministry as a result.

10. Your Website. Many churches encourage people to start thinking about starting a new ministry on their website. Here are several quotes right off churches' website:

"Ministries begin at Westwood Community Church through the initiative of Westwood attendees and/or staff. If you have the passion to begin a new ministry at Westwood, the process is outlined below..." (www.teamWestwood.org)

"Do you feel like God has placed a desire in you to start a new ministry at Southwest Community Church? We would love to help you build a ministry action plan for your new ministry by completing the following steps..." (www.Southwestcc.org)

"Saddleback has many ministries that have been started by lay ministers just like you. So, if you have a possible new ministry idea, please share it with us online so we can see if it qualifies as a new ministry." (www.Saddlebackfamily.com)

"Do you feel the desire to start a new ministry at Miracle Temple Church? We would love to help you..." (www.miracletemple.net)

Make it a Team Effort

The task of listening for passion should be part of the job description of every class teacher, small group leader, music director, youth leader and committee chair in your church. Sensitize your leaders to the importance of "passion-listening" when you are together for leadership training events, officers' retreats, and deacon/elder orientation. It's really not hard. It's just a matter of alerting church leaders to listen for what deeply affects their people. What they care about. The things that are really big in their life, either by choice or default.

You won't have to listen very hard or look very far to get Heartbeat ideas. For example, the McClean Bible Church, in Washington, D.C., reaches more than 700 area families who have children with disabilities through its ACCESS ministry. The ministry began in 1966 from a church newsletter ad placed by a family looking for someone to help care for their child with special needs while they were in church. Today it is one of the premier disabilities ministries in the country.

Church leaders should be constantly aware of passions, concerns, and interests that might be seeds for a Heartbeat ministry. Make this passion-sensitivity an ongoing part of your church's philosophy of ministry, not just a once-a-year effort.

What to Do Once You've Found the Passion

It's actually not very hard to find people with passion in a church; many of whom want to do something about it. As you develop a side-door philosophy of ministry, people will come to you with their ideas and dreams. And that's the way it should be. So, now what?

The following flow chart visualizes a healthy sequence in birthing a new Heartbeat ministry. A brief description of each step follows the chart...

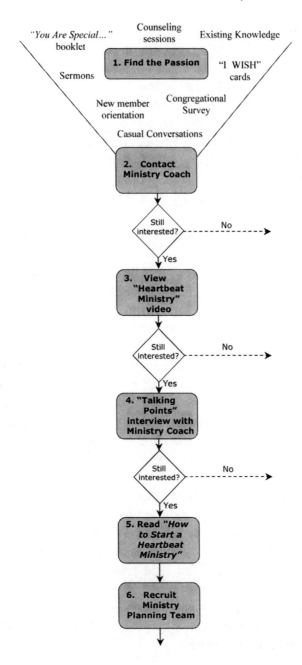

1. Find the Passion. Rick Warren recalls how their prayer ministry began: "A woman came up to me and said: 'We need a prayer ministry.' I said, 'I agree. You're it.' She said, 'Don't I have to be elected or go through some approval process?' She had imagined having to jump through all kinds of hoops first. I said, 'Of course not. Just announce a formation meeting in the bulletin and start it.' She did."[6] We have just suggested a variety of ways for how and where to find passion in your church. As the above diagram suggests, the more ways you have of communicating with members about pursuing their heartbeat, the better.

2. Contact Ministry Coach. Churches that create a "greenhouse" environment where members are released to pursue their passion, do not depend on the pastor to tend the greenhouse. Based on research of successful side-door churches, I recommend that every church (regardless of size) have a "go-to" person(s) who oversees the process of starting and nurturing new ministries. Alan Nelson, in his popular book, *From Me to We*, observes: "...every church should have someone (besides the pastor) who will champion the equipping value and develop ministry teams to implement the process."[7] I call this person a "Ministry Coach." Step Two in the above flowchart illustrates that as members respond to the idea pursuing personal interests in a Heartbeat ministry, they should contact the church's Ministry Coach. Chapter 15 provides a complete job description for this important role.

3. View "Heartbeat Ministry" CD. A 10-minute video called "Do You Have a Heartbeat?" introduces viewers to the idea of starting a Heartbeat ministry. Anyone in your church curious about starting a ministry around their passion should view this video. It is available online as a streaming video (www.HeartbeatMinistries.net), or it may be downloaded as a QuickTime file and then burned to a DVD. In this video viewers are encouraged to take five steps to explore whether God may be leading them to start a new ministry. Here is the transcript from this portion of the video concerning "Now what?"…

> *1. Reflect. What are the significant experiences in your life that have made you who you are. Ask yourself, "Are there things in my life that are really important to me? Things that I feel passionately about?" Perhaps there are certain challenges that have deeply affected you. Or, maybe you're passionate about a hobby or a past-time. Reflect on who you are, and what you really care about.*

> *2. Pray. Spend some serious time in the next several weeks asking God if he might be preparing you for something rather significant. A pastor once told me, "God doesn't waste our experience." Ask God to help you see the unique person that he has created in you, and whether there is a creative ministry which you might be uniquely qualified to spark.*

> *3. Dream. Let you mind go. Cast off limitations of time and money and ask yourself the question: "What might be an exceptional ministry in this area five years from today? What activities might be going on? Who might be touched? How might God's love and healing and community be experienced by the people who would come in contact with this ministry?"*

> *4. Talk. First, talk with some of your friends and family about the idea of a new ministry. What ideas do they have? Do you find your enthusiasm growing as you discuss these ideas? Sometimes God speaks to us through those around us. Then, if you're still energized by the idea of a creative new ministry in your church, make an*

appointment with your pastor or staff person to discuss the idea. We have provided a resource for you in this CD to help you prepare for the meeting. If you're watching this program on a computer, simply click on the link that says: "Talking Points" in the lower left corner of the screen. This will download a document that will help you organize your thoughts prior to meeting with your pastor or staff person. Finally…

5. Begin. If you decide to pursue the idea of a new ministry, your church has helpful materials to guide you through the process. For example, you will learn how to identify people in your church and community who may want to help in the new ministry. You'll receive a checklist with steps for starting a new ministry, along with guidelines with how and where to begin. You'll learn how to find churches around the country that have ministries similar to the one you're considering, so that you can learn from them. You'll have plenty of help in doing it right.

4. Hold a "Talking Points" Interview with the Ministry Coach. After viewing the video, if the lay person wants to continue exploring the idea of a new ministry, he/she should meet with the Ministry Coach or pastor/staff. A "Talking Points" discussion guide is provided in Appendix B that will help you focus on the issues involved in starting a new ministry. Ideally this discussion guide should be provided to the "visionary" prior to the meeting so that he/she can think about their responses to the questions. The "Talking Points" questions may also be downloaded as a .pdf file from: www. HeartbeatMinistries.net.

5. Read "How to Start a Heartbeat Ministry" workbook. If the conclusion of the "talking points" interview leads to a decision to proceed, the layperson should be given a copy of the workbook, "How to Start a New Ministry." This is a step-by-step guide that everyone starting a new ministry should use. It was developed based on research and experience of how new ministries are successfully started. Obviously everyone wants the new ministry to succeed, so it just makes sense to have the "builders" of this side-door read the "blue-print." A .pdf file of the workbook may be downloaded at the Heartbeat Ministry website (www.HeartbeatMinistries. net). Bound copies may also be ordered on the website. You have already read the Introduction and Chapter One in this workbook. Much of the remaining contents is included in Part II of this book.

6. Recruit a Ministry Planning Team. The first thing the church member is encouraged to do in the *How to Start a Heartbeat Ministry* workbook is to recruit a "Ministry Planning Team." This is a group of several people who share the passion and the dream, and will work as a team to start the new ministry. Don Cousins notes, "Once you find the key leader, assemble five or six individuals to brainstorm about the ministry. This 'think tank' typically consists of the ministry leader, several other people with a passion and gift-edness for the ministry, and one or two staff members or elders."[8]

Once the Ministry Planning Team has been identified, they should meet with the Ministry Coach. And, with that meeting, an exciting birth of a new Heartbeat ministry in your church has begun!

The Power of Side-doors

The New Life Church, in Colorado Springs, was started in 1985. Today the church has 8,700 members, four services, and over 800 groups. It is one of many growing churches that encourage members to build new side-doors around their passions (they call them "Free Market Groups"). In the book, *Dog Training, Fly Fishing, and Sharing Christ in the 21ˢᵗ Century* the author writes about a group of men from their church who get together every few weeks for fly fishing in the mountains west of Colorado Springs: "They talk, and laugh, and enjoy the beauty of the outdoors. But these guys aren't just out for a day of fly fishing. They aren't just recreating. In fact, they are holding an officially registered New Life Church small group."[9]

The author goes on to make an important point that applies to successful side-doors and Heartbeat ministries:

> While this group is meeting in the streams of the Rocky Mountains, back in town, other church groups are meeting. A dog training group gathers in the city park. Aspiring writers meet in a member's home to read and discuss their works. A financial expert coaches a group of young couples on money management. Men pour into a basketball gym for a pickup game. Women sit drinking coffee and discussing the latest best-selling book at a bagel shop.
>
> These don't look like church groups. But they are. They are ministry groups that have been planned, organized, and covered in prayer. Some of them may never pray or crack open the Bible, but they are an integral part of the ministry of the New Life Church. These groups are as important as Sunday services.
>
> This seems odd, right? After all, what do fly-fishing, dog training, and eating bagels have to do with sharing Christ? They are ministry. And this ministry perfectly expresses what the Bible is all about: loving God and loving others. When these men are grabbing their rods and boxes of lures to go fishing, the discussions they have will provide as much, or more, practical life coaching than many Sunday morning Bible class. I believe ministry is connecting

deeply with others. And connecting with others happens when we share ourselves, our interests, and our lives with people. While Christians in many churches share their time and lives with others in the church, a powerful insight into sharing Christ is for the church to help members connect with those outside the church, based around those same interests.[10]

While the pastor of a church can (and should) raise awareness ... identify opportunities ... encourage initiatives, eventually the pastor must step back and let the people pursue their passion. In so doing, the influence of Christ's love will begin flowing through the heartbeat of these people. And this process of enthusiasm and involvement in ministry significantly broadens the number of people who come into contact with Jesus Christ through the relationships that grow with Christ's followers. It is truly a contagious and exciting thing to experience!

chapter six

Build a Dream Team

> NOTE: Chapters 6 – 14 are adapted from the workbook,
> **How to Start a Heartbeat Ministry in Your Church**, which
> I wrote as a companion to this book. These chapters give
> step-by-step guidelines for starting a new ministry. They
> are included here to provide the reader with a better
> understanding of the steps involved in starting a heartbeat
> ministry. As you read these pages, remember that the word
> "you" is referring to the layperson(s) who is following this
> guide.

Starting a new ministry is not a marathon, it's a relay.
You can't—and shouldn't try to—do it alone.

Now that you have met with your pastor, staff member
or Ministry Coach, your next important step to beginning a
successful new ministry is to invite some people to join you
in two important areas:

1) Prayer
2) Planning

Here are some suggestions for finding the right people
in both areas:

Your Prayer Support Team

You will find it *very* helpful to have people praying for you during the important days of birthing the new ministry. Scripture tells us that the prayers of believers have great power and wonderful results (James 5:16). Your efforts will be more successful, your mind will be sharper, your heart will be softer when fellow Christians are asking God to bless you and your endeavors. There is no limit to the number of people you can ask for prayer support. But I recommend at least five people who have individually agreed to pray for you in the next several months. Ask these people to pray that God would grant you:

- *Vision* to see the potential of this ministry dream
- *Discernment* when choices are needed on how to proceed
- *Compassion* for the people who will be affected by the ministry
- *Resolve* if/when your patience or enthusiasm may falter

Here are some ideas of *who* you can ask to pray for you:

- friends (in or outside your church, at home or far away)
- relatives (same as above)
- your Sunday school class or small group
- your church intercessory prayer team
- other Christians who know and care about you

Your Ministry Planning Team

In the days ahead, the steps of birthing a new ministry won't always be easy. But that doesn't mean it won't be rewarding or worthwhile. In fact, it will likely be one of the most rewarding things you have done. In order to share both the challenges and the joys on your upcoming journey, you need to have a group of 2 – 4 people walking alongside you. This group is called your *Ministry Planning Team.*

Your Ministry Planning Team is composed of people who share your dream of starting a new ministry in and through your church. Here are some reasons why a Ministry Planning Team (MPT) is so important:

- It's more fun going on a journey with others who share your excitement.
- It's nice to have people to encourage each other when it's needed.
- It's easier to come up with good ideas as a group than on your own.
- It's just a more effective and efficient way to get things done.

Puppet Ministry
Grace United Methodist Church (Merritt Island, FL)
We have puppet team practice every Monday at 6:00 p.m. to 8:00 p.m. in the Music Room. Everyone is invited. Bring a friend. (from website)

A Ministry Planning Team is so important to the success of your new venture that if you can't find at least two other people to help you get started on this first stage of the journey, *you should not continue* until you find some. Here are two general groupings from whom you might invite people to join you on your pilgrimage:

Friends/relatives. If a spouse, family member, or other relative shares your enthusiasm with the idea, they can be helpful and fun to work with. Perhaps you have friends in your church who would be willing to help you get started and serve in your Ministry Planning Team.

Passionates. It is likely that there are people in your church who care about the same thing that has motivated you this far in exploring a new ministry. Ask your pastor or a staff member if there is anyone in the church who might be interested.

Initial Activities of the Ministry Planning Team

There are two activities that your MPT will be involved in immediately: 1) researching churches with similar ministries to what you are considering, and 2) defining the target audience who will be most affected by your new ministry. Below is a brief *description* of both activities. The next two chapters provide more detailed guidance for each step.

THE BLENDED BUNCH
What Mike and Carol Brady Never Knew

A Panel Discussion for Blended Families

Blended Family Ministry
Grace Community Church
Noblesville, IN)

*Blended Family Series:
7:00 p.m.- 8:30 p.m.
Topics: July 7— Family of Origin;
July 14—Sibling Rivalry;
July 21—Hidden Issues;
July 28—Setting Healthy
Boundaries. (website)*

1) <u>Researching churches with similar ministries</u>. There are many creative churches around the country that may already have a ministry similar to one you are considering. Knowing what these churches are doing and what they have learned will help you develop a ministry that is first-class right from the start. You will primarily be conducting Internet research of churches and then contacting leaders of these ministries to learn more about what they are doing. (The next chapter provides you with guidelines on how to conduct and compile your research.)

2) <u>Defining your target audience</u>. Your "target audience" is the collection of people (both in and outside your church) who will be potentially involved in your new ministry, or benefit from it. *The more narrowly you define your target group, the more likely your new ministry will be successful.* (Later you will define your target audience in a way that greatly increases your chances of success.)

Final Check Before Going On...

___ YES I have at least 5 people who have said they will pray for our efforts to begin a new ministry in our church. They are:

1. _____
2. _____
3. _____
4. _____
5. _____

___ YES I have 2-4 people who have agreed to serve on the "Ministry Planning Team" with me to help begin a new ministry in our church. They are:

1. _____
2. _____
3. _____
4. _____

chapter seven

Research Other Ministries

You've probably used, or at least heard, the old saying "let's not re-invent the wheel." It's good advice. There are many churches around the country with creative people and creative ministries, and you will do yourself a great favor to learn from them.

Your goal in this chapter is to: 1) research other churches on the Internet that have ministries related to your area of interest, 2) identify three churches that seem to be models of what you are considering, and 3) communicate with these three churches to learn more about their ministries, and then summarize your findings. This exercise will:

* give you helpful ideas for your own ministry
* save you from making avoidable mistakes
* prevent your waste of time and money
* help you communicate your dream to other leaders in your church
* energize you and your Ministry Planning Team (MPT) to see possibilities of what your own ministry might look like one day

Let's Get Started

Researching other churches is the first activity of your new Ministry Planning Team, and it will be an enjoyable one. You will be doing online research of churches with similar ministries as what you are considering.

Motorcycle Ministry
Harvest Christian Church
(Bakersfield, CA)

Our purpose is to allow the Holy Spirit to use our motorcycles and riding as a means to witness to the world, beginning with those in our local community.
(website)

Hopefully, at least one person on your MPT is familiar with using the Internet to do research using Google or another search engine. If no one on your MPT has Internet experience, ask a 12-year old in your church for help. (Little joke, there.) But you will need to find someone who can give you a short lesson, or work at the computer while you and the other members of your MPT look over his/her shoulder. You should be able to do most of your Internet research in one 2-hour session.

Plan a time at someone's home or a place where you have access to a high-speed Internet connection and a printer. Begin by entering one or more key words in the Internet search that reflect the area of your interest. You can, and should, use multiple words in one search. Be sure to use the word "church" as one of the searchable key words, since you are looking for churches that have ministries in the area of your focus. Another word you could try is "ministry." Experiment with different word combinations to see what kind of "hits" you get.

Your goal for this initial research is to find several dozen churches that have a ministry or activity related to your area of interest. Your long-term goal is to find three churches that have a ministry similar to the kind you are imagining, so that you can talk with them and learn from their experience. In this initial research, however, you simply want to search the Internet to see what you can find. To record the results of your search, use the format on the page entitled: "Initial Web Search" later in this chapter. (A downloadable copy is available at www.HeartbeatMinistries. net). Your completed page will help you identify three models that you can study later in more detail. And, you may want to refer back to some of these churches later as you move farther along in developing your ministry.

In your research, don't worry about whether the church...

Crisis Pregnancy Ministry
First Baptist Church
(Pearland, TX)

"If God has given you a passion for women in crisis and their babies, there are many volunteer opportunities available. You may contact the church office."
(website)

* *is larger than yours.* The process of starting and conducting a successful ministry is the same, regardless of church size. Most larger churches do things right, so there is much to learn from them.
* *has a different theology than yours.* It turns out that churches and ministries don't grow because of "right" or "wrong" theology, anyway. They grow because they are touching felt needs of people with and through God's love. And that's just what your new ministry will be doing!
* *is in a different location than yours.* Neither do churches grow because they are in a certain city or part of the country. A common misconception is that "such and such church is growing because they are in so and so part of the country or city." Don't believe

it. People are people, and people have the same interests and needs no matter where they live.

Boys to Men
Reid Temple AME Church
(Glenn Dale, MD)

Provides youth within Reid Temple and the surrounding community with dedicated adult mentors equipped with skills to encourage spiritual growth, self-esteem, social development, academic achievement, and career awareness.
(from website)

Also in your research, visit Amazon.com. Use similar search words or phrases as in your Google search. Here you are looking for related books, videos, or other resources of interest. If there is an author who has written on your topic, consider buying the book. Note whether he/she is associated with a church and whether you would want to contact the person for more information.

In your online research, you may also come across other information that will be helpful to you, such as articles, curriculum, websites, videos, nonprofit organizations, etc. Print out anything that looks helpful. For this reason, you should develop a 3-ring notebook and bring it with you on your research night. Buy a set of 8 divider tabs for your notebook and label them:

Tab 1: Case #1: [fill in church name]
Tab 2: Case #2: [fill in church name]
Tab 3: Case #3: [fill in church name]
Tab 4: Ministries/Organizations
Tab 5: Websites
Tab 6: Articles
Tab 7: Books
Tab 8: People

Three Model Church Ministries

Once you and the MPT members feel you have adequately researched your area of interest, select three churches that seem to have a particularly effective ministry. Divide these case study churches among the members of your MPT. The assignment is to contact the case study churches and schedule a telephone interview between your MPT and someone at each church who is knowledgeable about that ministry. A sample "Ministry Case Study" report form is provided later in this chapter to help you summarize each model church ministry. (A downloadable copy is available at www.HeartbeatMinistries.net.)

Here are the steps for researching each of the three church models:

1. **Schedule a telephone interview.**
   a. Your first call to the church is simply to set up a phone appointment. Ask to speak with the person (or their assistant) listed on the website who is responsible for the ministry in which you are interested. If you can't find a name on the website, ask the receptionist to speak with the person who oversees that ministry. Once you are transferred, introduce yourself as being from so-and-so church, and explain that you are hoping to begin a new ministry for such-and-such a target group. Explain that you found their church in your research and were hoping to set up a telephone appointment to speak with someone who would be willing to answer a few questions about that particular ministry. Mention that there are several others on your planning team who will be participating in the conference call. Also, mention that you would not expect the call to take longer than 20 minutes.

  b. Set a date and time for the call, and communicate this information to the members of the MPT.

2. Hold the conference call.

Before your call:

  a. Be familiar with your telephone system and how to set up a conference call. Get all your MPT members on the line five minutes before you call the church.

  b. With your MPT, review the information you already have on the church, as well as the questions you want to cover. (See the "Ministry Case Study" form at the end of this chapter.)

  c. One person on your end should be the "spokesperson" to moderate the interview, although any of the MPT members should feel free to ask questions. Be sure at least one person in your group is taking notes during the interview.

When you call:

  a. Thank the person you are calling for their graciousness in giving this time for the interview. Introduce each person on your MPT who is participating in the conference call.

  b. Use the "Ministry Case Study" to guide the interview. But don't feel limited if there are other questions you would like to ask.

  c. Your conversation should last no longer than 20 – 25 minutes. When finished, again thank the person for their time.

After you call:

  a. Debrief the conversation with your MPT members. Go over the questions from the "Ministry Case Study" form and share your various perspectives on each question.

b. One member of the MPT should be responsible for writing up the case study by completing the "Ministry Case Study" pages in more detail.

c. Repeat this phone interview process with two other churches.

3. **Consider a church visit.**

a. If any of the three case studies seem like examples of the dream you have for your own ministry, consider actually visiting the church and observing some of their activities first-hand. If you decide to go, schedule your visit around their calendar so you will see the ministry in action. You may also want to schedule appointments for when you are there with one or more leaders of the ministry. If the church you are visiting is in Southern California, and you are going in mid-February, consider it as just one of the prices you'll have to pay!

Initial Web Search

Create a page like this to record the results of your Internet search:

Church Name	City/ST	Web Home Page	Comments

Ministry Case Study

Church Name: _____
Church Address: _____
Church Phone: (_____) _____
Church Website: www._____
Average Weekend Attendance: _____ Number of Services: _____
Day/Time of Services: _____
Year the Church Started: _____ Denomination: _____
Name of Ministry: _____
Ministry Website (if different from church): www._____

Date of Phone Interview: _____
With: _____ Title: _____
Your Name: _____

How and when did the ministry begin?

Does the ministry have a written purpose statement? (Obtain a copy if possible.)

What kind of activities does the ministry engage in? What comments do you have about these activities?

MINISTRY ACTIVITY	COMMENTS BY INTERVIEWEE

Are there plans for expanding the ministry? If so, in what ways?

What obstacles or challenges were encountered in the birth or growth of this ministry?

How were they handled?

What suggestions do you have about how to avoid these problems, or what to do if they are encountered?

Are you aware of any resources that would be helpful to us in this area?

    Books:

    Organizations/People:

    Websites:

    Churches with similar ministries:

    Seminars, conferences, etc.:

Do you have any other comments or suggestions that would be helpful to us in starting a similar ministry in our church?

chapter eight

Define Your Target Audience

Your ministry will be most effective if you begin with a clear understanding of exactly *who* will be touched by it. This may sound obvious, but a clear definition of your target audience is very important in the successful birthing of a new ministry. Mark Howell, founder of SmallGroupResources. net, says that clearly defining your target audience is "very big." Launching a new Heartbeat ministry "...without understanding who the ministry is designed to serve almost always leads to a miss."[1] The purpose of this chapter is to help you define and describe your target audience.

Leith Anderson summarizes the process of target group outreach: 1) *Define* who is to be reached; 2) *Learn* about these people; 3) *Determine* the most effective means of connecting with and reaching them.[2] In this chapter we will look at Anderson's first two points: 1) defining the target group, and 2) learning more about these people. In the next chapter we will focus on 3) determining the most effective means of connecting with and reaching them.

Let's Get Specific

Here is a principle that is critical to starting a successful new ministry:

The more specifically you define your target audience, the more likely your ministry will be successful.

For example, compare these two target group descriptions and see which one would catch your interest if it described you:

• Women
• Women between 25 – 40, who are divorced, with children living at home, who are facing financial difficulties.

The first group includes over half the population in your church and community. One might think that with so many potential participants it would be easy to get a crowd. In reality, it's just the opposite. Such a broad definition makes it nearly impossible to provide a need-meeting ministry to everyone who happens to be a woman.

The second target group is quite specific. It is easy to imagine the needs and an appropriate response that a need-meeting ministry would provide. If you were a person in this second target group, you would certainly be interested in learning more about a group or activity that could help make your quality of life better. And you would likely bond very quickly to other women in that group in similar life situations.

More Than Meets the Eye

As you identify the people in your target group, realize that there may well be more than just one group of people affected by your ministry. For example, Messiah Lutheran Church, in Yorba Linda, California, has a wonderful ministry called "Homework House." This is a ministry where adults tutor students who are "at risk" for not progressing in school. The initial target audience of this ministry is obviously kids having difficulty in school. But are there other people affected by this ministry? What about the parents and families of the children being tutored? How about the non-members of Messiah who are helping tutor the kids and are working hand-in-hand with Messiah church members? Are these "people groups" affected by the ministry? Of course!

On the other hand, Messiah also has a ministry called "Stork Support," which brings meals into homes during the hectic, sleep-deprived time when mom and the new baby first come home from the hospital. In this case, the target group is the new parents and their family, with no one else directly affected by this ministry.

Tutoring Ministry
Rosewood Christian Reformed Church (Bellflower, CA)
A free tutoring service to the children of our community in an atmosphere of care and love. The children are referred by Thomas Jefferson Elementary School.

So, before you go on, take a moment on the grid below to (in the left column) describe your *target group*; that is, the primary beneficiaries of your new ministry. You may not know the answer to each item, but consider all the relevant characteristics of your target audience. Remember, the more specifically you define these people, the more effectively you will be able to connect with them.

Next, consider whether there are others directly affected by the new ministry. Identify and describe these people in the second column.

	Your Target Audience	**Others Affected**
Age (range):		
Marital Status:		
Family Status:		

Interests/Hobbies:		
Concerns/Problems:		
Ethnic/Cultural Identity:		
Financial Status:		
Other Characteristics:		

Learning More About Your Target Audience

One of the most effective ways that professional marketing companies learn about their target audiences—and thus

Infant Loss Support Group
Calvary Lutheran Church
(Minneapolis, MN)

Safe, confidential place in a Christian context, to talk and listen to others experiencing these difficulties. Information, resources, care, and encouragement. You are not alone...

how to connect with them—is a research process called "focus groups."[3] It is a process you can (and should) apply in learning more about your own target group. Wikipedia defines the focus group process as: "a form of qualitative research in which a group of people is asked about their attitude towards a product, service, concept, advertisement, idea, or packaging. Questions are asked in an interactive group setting where participants are free to talk with other group members." Here are the components of a good focus group:

* Comprised of 8 - 10 people who represent the target audience
* The group meets for approximately one hour
* The group is led by an impartial moderator
* A set of appropriate questions has been formulated prior to the meeting

* The session is tape recorded, with participants' knowledge and permission

The goal of a focus group is to learn the thinking patterns and decision-making process of people in your target audience. It will take some time, planning, and effort to conduct a focus group. But it is an amazingly enlightening process for obtaining accurate information on the needs and concerns of your target audience. (Otherwise, so many professional business and research groups wouldn't be doing it!) And, once you have obtained such information on your target group, your ministry will be much more effective in connecting with their real needs. Consequently, I strongly recommended your MPT organize several focus groups with your target audience(s).

Here is a scenario with a research focus group that will help you better understand the process and its value:

You are planning a ministry for grandparents who are raising grandchildren. You are in such a situation yourself, and realize it is definitely a challenge. You know of at least one other family in the church, as well as two families from your grandchild's 3ʳᵈ grade class at school, who are in a similar situation. After speaking with your pastor about your interest, you have recruited a Ministry Planning Team of two other women in church. You are thinking that some kind of support group could be helpful to these families, but you thought that you might get a better idea of the real felt needs of this target audience if you could hear from them directly.

You have developed a flyer inviting anyone who has grandchildren in their home to participate in a 1-hour research interview, and to call your phone number for more information. You have distributed the flyer to people at church and asked them to give a copy to anyone they know in this kind of family situation. You have also mailed out 500 flyers, and run an ad in the "personals" section of the classified ads in your local newspaper.

Each person who is invited to participate receives $35 for their time. Childcare has been arranged. You have reserved a meeting room at the local library, and have eight people committed to the meeting at 7:00 p.m., and another seven attending a second focus group meeting at 8:15 p.m.

The room is set up with two 8' tables forming a square, and eight chairs around the tables. Coffee, soft drinks, and cookies are provided for participants before the meeting.

When the meeting begins you introduce yourself, thank the people for attending, and tell them they will receive their stipend at the end of the meeting. You explain that the goal is to solicit input from participants about the process and related issues of raising grandchildren. You encourage group members to be free in sharing their thoughts and opinions, and assure them that their comments will remain anonymous.

You have arranged for a small hand-held tape recorder to be placed in the center of the table, and explain that the purpose is to be sure everyone's comments are accurately recorded for future reference. You tell the group that after the comments have been transcribed the tape will be erased. Participants sign an agreement which allows their comments to be recorded.

You ask the first of six questions you have prepared. The hour goes quickly and you find participants are animated and engaged in the conversation. There seems to be a genuine interest in the topic, and several people actually volunteer their help in the future if you need it. Some of the insights and "hot buttons" mentioned by the group include:

- concerns about discipline in the home
- relations with their children (the grandchildren's parents)
- desire for grandkids' to have help with their homework
- desire for family recreation vs. their own failing health
- nurturing sibling relationships

At the conclusion of the meeting you thank participants for attending and give them an envelope with a $35 remuneration.

The second group begins to arrive just as the first group is finishing. You give the same introduction and ask for permission to record their comments. Interestingly, there are different comments and ideas that grow out of this second group, even though participants of both groups are raising grandchildren.

In this group there are several widows. One brings up the question of security of the kids at an event, since she is worried about their father picking them up without permission. Another is concerned about getting the kids to school and back home on days when she is sick or has a doctor's appointment. Again, several participants volunteer their help. One of the men said he is on the board of a local philanthropic foundation and could help in preparing a proposal for funding support. Another person says that she is on the school board, and is certain that the district would be supportive if the church were to start an after-school homework club.

As you are cleaning up after the meetings, you and the other members of the Ministry Planning Team are excited about both the positive input, and the connections you made with people who could help put this new ministry "on the map."

John and Shelley McKay

It can be helpful to create a "personality profile" of one or more people who typify your target audience. Describing your group in this way helps personalize certain characteristics into "real" people. Such a characterization will also help others in your church more easily understand and visualize the people on whom who your new initiative is focused. You can even give the person(s) a name!

If there may be more than one "typical" person in your target audience, develop several different personality profiles. And, if there is an important related group that will be affected by your new ministry, develop a profile for a person(s) in that group, as well. Below, complete a "personality profile" for a person in your ministry's target audience(s).

Typical Person #1:

Typical Person #2

For more information and guidance in conducting successful focus groups, refer to "Planning Your Focus Groups" in Appendix C. Then, as a Ministry Planning Team, discuss the process of conducting several focus groups in the coming month. Once you have competed the focus groups, write a one-page summary of what you learned and how your findings affect the mission and purpose of the new ministry. Following this, it is a good idea to meet with your pastor and/or Ministry Coach and brief them on your progress to date.

chapter nine

Define Your Purpose

The first step in constructing a solid building is the foundation. Huge skyscrapers can be built on a firm foundation. Yet, a small one-story house collapses under inadequate groundwork. So too, if your new ministry is going to be strong, you must have a strong foundation. That foundation is your "mission." Defining the purpose of a ministry is not time consuming, but it is important.

What's Our Real Purpose?

A mission statement for your ministry must reflect the mission of your church, since it is a ministry of your church. And, backing up one step farther, the mission statement of a church should reflect the mission of Christ, since Christ is the head. Because of this "square one" issue, it is worth a look at the question, "what was the mission of Christ?"

In Luke 19:10, Jesus said, "I have come [his mission] to seek and to save those who are lost." Later, in his final words to the disciples, and to those of us who

Clown Ministry
New Life United Methodist Church
(Midlothian, VA)

Our Ministry presently consists of eight Clowns. Our goal is to be encouragers, teachers, nurturers, and ministers of Jesus Christ's unconditional love to all people and for all people. (web site)

would follow, Jesus gave us our mission: "...go, therefore, and make disciples of all people. Teach them to obey everything I have told you..." (Matt. 28:19-20).

The *mission* of the church is often called "the great commission" ...to go and make disciples.

So, if that is the mission, what is the *method*? I suggest that the method is found in Mark 12:29-31, often called "the great commandment." When Jesus spoke these words, he had just been asked what was the most important thing we should do. His response—to love God as much as we can, and then to love others as much as we do ourselves.

Blind Ministry
First Lutheran Church
(Boston, MA)
We offer blind and visually impaired people opportunities for fellowship, Bible study, and Christian teaching on a variety of topics. Additionally, we offer educational opportunities to learn how to read and write Braille, as well as training in computer-related skills.

Hopefully your church's mission statement reflects some aspect of Christ's goal of making disciples—through love. If so, the mission statement of your new ministry should start out with this same foundation.

Another way of looking at your mission statement is this: It is simply the answer to the question, "*what* are we doing...*why* are we doing it...and *how* are we doing it?"

Do you remember when you completed the "Talking Points" discussion guide and went over the answers with your pastor or Ministry Coach? Here was one of the questions:

"A key part of considering new groups and ministries in our church is the potential for connecting with, and reaching out to, new and unchurched people. How do you see that occurring in this new ministry?"

Do you remember how you responded? It's an important question, because your new ministry needs to include those who are not yet part of the church and/or Christian faith. Todd Pridemore, an expert in starting Heartbeat ministries in his church, says: "Make sure everyone understands the primary purpose of this new ministry: reaching unchurched people. It is extremely easy for this new activity to evolve into nothing more than a fellowship group or social club for church members."[1]

A focus that includes those outside the church puts your new ministry solidly in line with Christ's own mission and that of your church. Of course, your ministry should not be exclusively outward-focused. There should be some of your own church members involved, as well. But, if the group is made up entirely of Christians and church members, it will become a diversion of the resources of your church away from its primary mission.

Sample Purpose Statements

Here are some purpose statements of effective Heartbeat ministries in churches around the country. Notice how: 1) they clearly define their target audience, and 2) they are designed to include people outside their church.

> *Hopekeepers* is a group for those dealing with a recent medical diagnosis, chronic illness and/or pain. Together we share prayer requests and questions. Meetings are held twice a month and are open to all friends and family. **Lake Avenue Church Pasadena, California**

> The goal of the *Crisis Care Ministry* is to provide assistance and resources to individuals in crisis—within and outside of PEPC—and to help them gain independence, self-sufficiency, and a closer spiritual relationship with Christ. "Crisis" is defined as an acute situation

requiring immediate assistance. **Parker Evangelical Presbyterian Church Denver, Colorado**

Pump-N-Praise is a 50-minute aerobic exercise program suited for women of most abilities and choreographed to contemporary Christian music. From warm up to cool down, participants listen to positive, life-affirming words to strengthen the spirit while we stretch, dance, and tone up our body. Share prayer requests and praises at the end of each class as we exercise the power of prayer. **Wheaton Bible Church Wheaton, Illinois**

Nathaniel's Hope is a ministry dedicated to sharing hope with kids with special needs (VIP kids) and their families. This includes:

- Bringing hope and encouragement to VIP kids and families through support groups and special activities

- Providing practical assistance by offering "Buddy Break," a free respite care for the caregivers of VIP kids every other Saturday morning

- Educating our church and community on how to be a Buddy to VIP kids and their families

- Sharing support and hope with grieving families **Calvary Assembly of God Orlando, Florida**

CRUISE Motorcycle Ministry leads fellow bikers and motorcycle enthusiasts toward a closer relationship with Jesus Christ and each other. Our mission is to ride safely as a group in Christian fellowship, and as an outreach team for our Lord. **Hickory Grove Baptist Church Charlotte, North Carolina**

Break Free is a ministry of hope and healing from the isolation, anxiety, fear, and shame that accompany chemical dependency. The ministry provides an opportunity for people to participate in a Christ-centered, 12-step process that is biblically based, non-denominational, clinically tested, and proven to provide important tools which an addicted person needs to make a complete recovery from chemical addiction. **Grove City Nazarene Church Columbus, Ohio**

Now take a few moments to develop a clear purpose statement for your envisioned ministry. A good way to develop your mission statement is for each member of your Ministry Planning Team to first write down their own ideas on the purpose of the ministry. Then, after each person has written something down, read the statements to each other. Finally, compile your respective ideas into one paragraph and write it below:

Our Mission Statement:

chapter ten

Plan Your Strategy

Now the fun begins. You are about to develop your plans for launching your new ministry! But first, look how far you've come. You have...

✓ assembled a group of people who are praying for and working with you in the process of pursuing a dream
✓ studied churches with similar ministries so as to make your initial efforts more effective
✓ defined your target audience—the people who will benefit from the new ministry
✓ written a mission statement of what you'll be doing, why, and how

Now, as you begin to define the scope of your new ministry, this chapter will help you organize your goals and strategy.

As with your other activities, you will want to complete this chart together as a Ministry Planning Team. It may take several meetings before you are

Sports Ministry
Southport Presbyterian Church (Indianapolis, IN)
The sports ministry exists to provide wholesome athletic experiences for the whole family and either introduce or further educate people about Jesus Christ.

satisfied with the outcome, but once you have completed it, you will be well on your way to realizing an exciting new ministry in your church.

NOTE: 1) Before you begin filling in your "Ministry Planning Chart" read this entire chapter, since it explains the chart and your related activities; 2) Copy the chart onto a piece of butcher paper or flipchart so you will have more room to write.

Ministry Planning Chart

		Target Audience	Others Affected
	Description:		

		Target Audience	Others Affected
Stage One **FELT NEEDS**	**1. Felt Need/s** of our Target Audience:		
	2. Our Goal/s that will respond to their felt needs:		
	3. The Process for achieving our goals:		
Stage Two **DEEPER NEEDS**	**1. Our Goal:**	*"To build increasingly meaningful and caring relationships among those touched by the ministry (church members and non-members)."*	
	2. The Process:		
Stage Three **ETERNAL NEEDS**	**1. Goal:**	*"To help those affected by the ministry to grow in their understanding and experience of God's love."*	
	2. Process:		

The remainder of this chapter discusses each of the cells on the above "Ministry Planning Chart."

TARGET AUDIENCE DESCRIPTION

There are two vertical halves to the "Ministry Planning Chart." The left half applies to your target audience—the people for whom your new ministry is designed. The right half applies to others who will be indirectly affected by the new ministry. In the example used earlier, if your dream is to start an after-school tutoring ministry, your target group would be the children who are struggling academically. However, the parents will obviously be affected by your new ministry and should also be considered in your ministry planning. On the chart you would list the kids in the description of your "Target Audience," and list the parents/guardians in the same row below "Others Affected." (If you are planning a new ministry in which the only group affected will be your target audience, leave the right half blank.) In either case, remember to be as specific as possible when describing the people who will be affected by your new ministry.

STAGE ONE: *FELT NEEDS*

On the Ministry Planning Chart you can see three major areas for your planning: Stage One, Two, and Three. In Stage One you will have three concerns: "Felt Need/s," "Our Goal/s," and The Process."

Hula Ministry
Saddleback Community Church
(Lake Forest, CA)

Our purpose: To minister hula as worship and share God with others through Christian lyrics, songs with Hawaiian style dancing. (website)

1) Identify the **FELT NEED/S** of your Target Audience. This is where your earlier research will come in handy, par-

ticularly the information from your focus groups. (You *did* do your focus groups, right?) Review your research and list one or more of the most important felt needs of the people in your target audience. Getting this right is very important. If you don't correctly identify a significant felt need of your target group, you will end up planning an activity which no one is interested in…and no one attends. Keep in mind that many start-up groups and ministries have failed due to an inaccurate assessment of the important felt needs of their target audience.

Covenant Bowling League
Covenant Community Church
(Orange, CA)
Started in 1983 by three members, the league now has 16 teams of 4 people. Participants enjoy good fellowship with both members and non-members. (website)

On the right half of the chart list the important felt needs of others who will be affected by your ministry.

Earlier we mentioned the "Homework House," a ministry of Messiah Lutheran Church, that is focused on tutoring academically needy children. Their research indicated that the felt needs of these kids (their target group) were: 1) a desire to be successful in school, 2) a fear of being called "stupid" by classmates, and 3) a sense of insecurity and a lowering self-image. The felt needs of the parents ("Others Affected") included: 1) a concern for their children's academic performance, 2) lack of time to help their children with homework, and 3) a desire to see their children develop strong self-esteem.

2) <u>Set one or more specific **GOALS** that will respond to the felt needs of your target audience.</u> In the case of the "Homework House" ministry, their goal was to establish an after-school tutoring program from 3:00 p.m. – 5:00 p.m. on

Monday through Thursday. Their goal for "Others Affected" (on the right side of the Ministry Planning Chart) was to develop a presentation that would introduce parents to the tutoring program so they would feel comfortable giving permission for the kids to attend. The presentation would specifically address the three felt needs they identified among parents.

3) <u>Identify the **PROCESS** by which your goals will be reached</u>. This is simply answering the question: "How do we get from here to there?" On the following page is a "Planning Worksheet" that one church developed to organize their planning process. It is helpful because it lets you identify all of the individual tasks involved in reaching your goal. At the top of this page write the description of your target group. Then list the goal that you just identified (see #2 above). Below that, write all the action steps that must be taken to reach the goal. Across from each action step write *when* the task should be completed, *who* is responsible for overseeing that particular task, and *how much* that step will cost. This "Planning Worksheet" has helped many churches break down a seemingly daunting task into manageable steps. (Downloadable copies are available at <u>www. HeartbeatMinistries.net</u>)

Planning Worksheet

TARGET GROUP: _____

Goal:			
Action Steps ("What")	**Deadline** ("When")	**Person Responsible** ("Who")	**Cost** ("How much")
1.	1.	1.	1.
2.	2.	2.	2.
3.	3.	3.	3.
4.	4.	4.	4.

STAGE TWO: *DEEPER NEEDS*

Your First Stage goal for the new ministry is to provide an event or group or activity which people want to attend because it speaks to an important felt need in their life. It may be a support group for women whose husbands are alcoholics. It may be a softball team that provides a place for recreation and fun. Whatever it is, the activity is designed to address a felt need of people in your target audience.

But your new ministry has the potential to go far beyond just meeting a felt need. While felt needs are real and important to people, and motivate action in order to resolve them, felt needs are generally short-term. When their need is met, they will lose interest and drift away...unless a deeper connection exists. Your new ministry has the potential for touching the essence of the human spirit, and providing longer-term benefits to people's deeper needs. "Stage Two" in your planning urges you to look beyond responding to people's immediate needs, and ask: "Can we bring a longer-term value to people's lives?"

Movers & Shakers Ministry
Perimeter Church
(Atlanta, GA)
The "Movers & Shakers" Furniture Ministry distributes donated furniture and appliances to those in need throughout our community. Further, we desire to extend a hand of friendship, pray for, and serve each of our recipients, donors, and volunteers. (website)

You have probably heard the phrase, "Give a man a fish, and he will eat for a day. Teach a man to fish, and he will eat for a lifetime." In a sense, that is what your ministry can do for people as you move on to Stage Two. "Giving a person a fish" is what you are doing at Stage One when you are focusing on meeting their short-term felt needs. That is good, and important. But "teaching a person to fish" is what you do at Stage Two and Three. You will be enhancing their lives for the long-term.

The question: "What are people's deeper needs?" The answer revolves around one word: "Relationships." Stage Two helps you to focus on strengthening the inter-personal relationships between the people in your new ministry.

1) <u>Your **Goal** in Stage Two is to build relationships</u>. On the "Ministry Planning Chart" I have already suggested the wording for your **Goal** in Stage Two: "To build increasingly meaningful and caring relationships among those affected by your new ministry (both church members and non-members)".

Solomon spoke often of the value of friendship...

❖ *"By yourself, you're unprotected. With a friend, you can face the worse. Can you round up a third? A three-stranded rope isn't easily snapped."* (Ecc. 4:12 MS)

❖ *"Just as lotions and fragrance give sensual delight, a sweet friendship refreshes the soul."* (Prov. 27:9 MS)

❖ *"Better a nearby friend than a distant family."* (Prov. 27:10 MS)

2) <u>Determine the **PROCESS** by which relationships will grow</u>. This book is not the place for a detailed discussion on how to create and nurture meaningful relationships. But, there is much to be learned about nurturing relationships that last a lifetime. Here I would like to share with you an insightful list of five deeper human needs. Look at this list and ask how each of these deeper human needs can be met among the people who become involved in your new ministry. When you can help people meet these needs you will have begun a powerful process of fostering valued and caring friendships.

Needs of People Today

1. People feel disconnected and isolated, they are looking for a <u>place to belong</u> and feel part of a family or community.

2. People are feeling the pressure of a busy and stressful world. They are looking for a greater <u>sense of balance</u> and ways to manage priorities.

3. People sense the shallowness of superficial encounters with others. They are looking for <u>authentic relationships</u>.
4. People are feeling empty and drained from striving to meet their desires through work, material possessions, or entertainment. They are looking for <u>spiritual answers</u> to their unfulfilled "hunger."
5. People are feeling overwhelmed by the pace of change in every aspect of their world. They are looking for <u>help through transitions</u>.

STAGE THREE: *ETERNAL NEEDS*

Stage Three is actually not so much an entirely different idea, as an extension of the Second Stage to a deeper level. It is a progression from friendships…to love. It is the process of helping people experience God's love through the love of God's people.

Dulcimer Club
Rock Hill Baptist Church
(Beaumont, TX)
Bring your acoustic instrument (Dulcimer, Guitar, Banjo, Autoharp, Mandolin, Harmonica) and join the party!

I came across the following quote on an Internet blog by an anonymous "Missional Pastor":[1] "What I have noticed in the church is that when people start to get to know each other they begin to care for one another. When people care for one another with genuine affection then they learn to lean upon each other and perhaps even start to grow together in the Lord." I suspect the blogger was talking about people in his church. However, this same dynamic happens even when Christians and non-Christians come together: they get to know each other…they begin to care for each other...they lean upon each other...they grow in (and toward) the Lord with each other.

1) <u>Your **Goal** in Stage Three is to help people experience God's love</u>. In Stage Three of your Ministry Planning Chart I suggest the following goal: "To enable those affected by your ministry to grow in their understanding and experience of Gods' love." Your question, in planning the process of achieving this goal, is "What can we do to help people come to experience the genuine presence of God and His love?" It is a critically important question because, when it's all said and done, the Christian faith and its influence in our lives can be summed up in one word..."love." Christianity is basically God's love for us, and our love for God expressed through our love for others (see Matt. 22:37-40).

If the unchurched people who are part of your ministry/group can really come to believe that they can be loved—by a personal God and by God's personal family—they have taken a giant step toward establishing their own personal relationship with that God of love. Bob Bast, in the book *Attracting New Members,* correctly observes that most non-Christians "...already know they are sinners. They don't need to be convinced of that. What they doubt, or cannot believe, is the reality and depth of God's love for them. That note of grace—of unconditional love—needs to be experienced before it can be believed."[2]

2) <u>Determine the **PROCESS** by which people will experience God's love</u>. When the Christians in your new ministry become "open channels" for God's love to flow through them to those who are not Christians or church members, a powerful "love line" is established. "They will know you are Christians by your love."

Here are guidelines for helping people learn to love, from my book *Who Cares About Love?*[3] For an excellent resource to teach and learn more about being a channel for God's love to those around us, see *Growing in Love,*[4] a 13-week course that is easily taught by a lay or staff church leader.

1. *Learn and Practice the Skills of Listening.* Eye contact, body language, asking questions, giving feedback all improve our connections with people, because they communicate that we care.
2. *Deepen Your Level of Communication.* The kind of communication we have affects our relationship with people. Here are four levels of communication, moving from superficial to intimate:
    ♦ Exchange of clichés
    ♦ Exchange of information
    ♦ Exchange of opinions
    ♦ Exchange of emotions
    The more we appropriately share our opinions and emotions, the more we invest in our relationships. The closer people feel to us, and we to them.
3. *Practice empathy.* Here's a great insight about empathy from Atticus Finch in the classic book, *To Kill a Mockingbird*:
    "If you just learn a single trick, Scout, you'll get along a lot better with all kinds of folks. You never really understand a person until you understand things from his point of view...until you climb inside of his skin and walk around in it."
    Jesus says it only slightly different:
    "Here is a simple rule of thumb for behavior: Ask yourself what you want people to do for you; then grab the initiative and do it for them!" (Luke 6:31 The Message)
4. *Identify a Need in the Person's Life.* As we spend more time listening to a person (#1 above), and communicating with them at a deeper level (#2), we can begin to see the world from their perspective (#3). By so doing,

we become more aware of the person's need/s. Needs may be:

♦ Physical
♦ Emotional
♦ Relational
♦ Spiritual

5. *Respond with an Appropriate, Caring Gift.* Receiving a meaningful gift is one of the highlights of life. Giving such a gift is certainly one of the most powerful ways of showing love. This step comes naturally when we understand a person's needs (#4).

A good gift is not necessarily something purchased. The gift of time... or respect... or forgiveness can be most appropriate. Stanley Mooneyham once observed: "Love spoken can be turned aside. Love demonstrated is irresistible."[5]

A good gift is:

♦ *Meaningful*, based on the needs of the person receiving it
♦ *Sacrificial*, or it is just a convenience
♦ *Unexpected*, rather than predictable due to protocol
♦ *Unconditional*, with no expectation of return

"In lives increasingly experienced via monitors," observes Michael Johnson, "there is a hunger for genuine empathy and direct personal contact. People are attracted by churches that respond to their God-created inner need—a deeply embedded inner desire—to experience community, authentic relationship, and the mystery of love."[6]

chapter eleven

Publicize Your Ministry

When you have the first gathering of your new ministry, wouldn't it be nice to have people show up? Yet we've all been to meetings that have had a disappointing turn out despite an excellent program. A good meeting with poor attendance—especially when it's your first gathering—is no fun. In fact, it can be downright discouraging.

So, this chapter has some important suggestions for getting a crowd at your first—and subsequent—meetings.

First, let's review the "target audience" you will be inviting to attend your event. Keep in mind that there are *two* distinct groups within your target audience: 1) those who are presently IN your church, and 2) those who are NOT. Both groups are important. The more challenging group, as you can imagine, is communicating with and involving those who are not a part of your church. But remember, our goal is that 25%-75% of the participants are non-members. And, it is this group that is most important to the success of your new ministry. The focus groups and other research you did earlier will be helpful as you plan your publicity. To begin, write and review a brief description of your target audience:

```
┌─────────────────────────────────────────────────┐
│ OUR TARGET AUDIENCE:                            │
│                                                 │
│                                                 │
│                                                 │
│                                                 │
│                                                 │
│                                                 │
│                                                 │
└─────────────────────────────────────────────────┘
```

Strategies for Getting a Crowd

Here are five helpful insights about marketing that will help you publicize your new ministry, especially your first meeting. Below each strategy is a space for your Ministry Planning Team to write down action steps you can take to apply these strategies to your situation.

STRATEGY #1: *Decide why the benefit is worth the price*

People who consider attending your event will be subconsciously asking the question: "What is the benefit and what is the cost?" "What is the promise and what is the price?" As you write publicity material for your new ministry, *highlight the benefits* of attending. Or, as someone once said, "sell the sizzle." Effective promotion will convince prospective attendees that their risk of attending is worth the benefit they will receive. It's a simple mental equation in their mind: if the promise is worth the price they will attend; if not, they won't. One of the greatest "costs" most people have is *time*. Their schedules are full, at least in their own mind, and most people are not looking for one more thing to do. So the big question you need to answer in your publicity is, "Why should I re-arrange my schedule to attend your meeting?"

In the grid below, list the benefits of attending (from your prospective attendees' point of view). "Why will it be worth my time to go?" Then list the "costs" they will have to pay to attend (i.e., discomfort, time, transportation, etc.).

	Unchurched	Churched
Benefits of Attending		
Costs of Attending		

STRATEGY #2: *Produce a nice color brochure*

The more people you want to attend your meetings, the nicer your brochure needs to be. The least desirable approach is to use clipart from a desktop publishing program and design a brochure yourself. A better approach is to buy several hundred pre-printed template brochures at a local stationery store, then add your own copy and print it on a laser printer. The best approach is to secure the services of a professional designer who can help you develop an attractive color brochure that "sells the sizzle" and invites people to the activity. Be sure to apply strategy #1 in writing the copy for your brochure.

What are the steps we will take to develop a nice brochure?

STRATEGY #3: *Personal invitations work better than mass invitations*

Experience tells us that a good mass mailing will generate approximately 1% return. That is, for every 100 flyers you send out, one person will show up. By contrast, personal invitations are closer to 30% return; for every 100 personal invitations given (from people who know each other), 30 will show up. Personal invitations are more effective, much cheaper, and involve more people in the promotional effort. You certainly need a nice flyer or brochure of your new ministry. But mass mailing a brochure should never take the place of a personal invitation. In fact, the best use of a brochure is to have it given to a friend by a friend.

Ask, and answer, the question: "How are we going to use personal invitations to get the word out?"

Unchurched Target Audience	Churched Target Audience

STRATEGY #4: *Provide for Multiple Exposures*

Your target audience should hear about the event more than once. In fact, the more often they hear about it, the more likely they will come. Research actually shows that a group of people can see/hear the same message up to seven times and with each exposure more people will respond.

Answer the question, "How are we going to get the message out multiple times?"

Unchurched Target Audience	*Churched Target Audience*

STRATEGY #5: *Use Multiple Media*

The *number of times* people hear a message is important (Strategy #4). But so is the *number of ways* people hear it. The more senses involved in receiving a message, the more likely it will be remembered. Some are auditory learners, some visual, some tactile. Be creative about different communication media you use to extend your invitation. Don't just send the same flyer three or four times. Be creative. Answer the question: "What different media are we going use to get invitations out?"

Unchurched Target Audience	Churched Target Audience

Radio Control Car Ministry
Church in the Farms (Jupiter, FL)
Using sports as common ground, the sports ministry groups share the gospel with people and families in our community.

Use the "Publicity Planning Worksheet" in this chapter to identify and schedule the tasks, people, and time required to publicize your event. If it appears that the time required to adequately publicize the event is more time than you have before the meeting...postpone the meeting. You don't have a second chance at a successful first meeting. And the success of that meeting will be important in establishing momentum for your ministry's future.

By the way, when you are listing people to help with publicity, think beyond your Ministry Planning Team. This is a great opportunity to broaden the number of people who might have an interest in the new ministry and want to help get the word out. And, be sure to invite people who are NOT part of your church.

Publicity Planning Worksheet

Proposed first meeting date: _____

People who can be invited to be a part of the publicity activities:

PUBLICITY TASK	PERSON RESPONSIBLE	DATE TO BE COMPLETED	COST
1.	1.	1.	1.
2.	2.	2.	2.
3.	3.	3.	3.
4.	4.	4.	4.

chapter twelve

Prepare For Your First Meeting

You don't have a second chance for a good first impression. Your first meeting, therefore, will be important to set the tone for future meetings. And, it will have a large impact on whether people decide to come back. Here we will consider the key preparation concerns to make your first gathering a good one.

<u>Hosts</u>. A good meeting should have a warm, friendly, comfortable atmosphere. To encourage this you should plan to have at least one person designated as a "host" for each 5-8 people you expect. Here's a brief job description for each host:

Alzheimer's Support Ministry
Southeast Christian Church
(Louisville, KY)
Our purpose is to help the caregiver be a "best friend" to their loved one with memory loss and find ways to take care of themselves. (website)

* Be at the meeting at least 30 minutes before the publicized starting time.
* Greet those who arrive and engage them in conversation. Invite newcomers

to have refreshments, and introduce them to others in the room.

* If people arrive alone and do not seem to know anyone, make an effort to spend time with these persons and introduce them to others.
* Mingle; don't spend all the time with one person.

We are expecting _____ people. Our hosts will be:

Nametags. The general rule is to use nametags until everyone knows each other. If the chances are good that you will have new people at each meeting, have nametags at each meeting. Simple peel-off nametags are the best and easiest. Have a supply on hand along with Sharpie pens. Hosts should wear a nametag and give them to people as they arrive.

Person responsible to bring nametags and pens

Room preparation. The room set up will depend on the kind of meeting you are planning and the number of people you expect.

However, the general principle is to arrange the room in a way that facilitates interaction. This would include chairs set up so people can see each other (horseshoe, round tables, circle, etc.). Don't put the chairs too close together that you intrude into people's psychological space.

> **Diagram of room set-up**
>
>
>
>
>
>
>
>

Refreshments. Have refreshments (coffee, drinks, cookies, etc.) when people arrive.

> **List of refreshments and person responsible**
>
>
>
>
>
>
>
>

Ice-Breaker. Hopefully there will be many people at the meeting who do not know each other. Relationships can be started with something as simple as a creative ice-breaker early in the meeting. There are many ideas available on the Internet. Choose an activity that does not take too long, but gets people talking and laughing. (It's a good idea to have an ice-breaker activity to begin each meeting.)

```
┌─────────────────────────────────────────────┐
│ Icebreaker and person to lead                 │
│                                               │
│                                               │
│                                               │
│                                               │
│                                               │
│                                               │
└─────────────────────────────────────────────┘
```

Getting acquainted. Have people introduce themselves at some point early in the meeting. Give them an idea of what they should say about themselves; don't make it too long or too personal.

```
┌─────────────────────────────────────────────┐
│ How will people introduce themselves?         │
│                                               │
│                                               │
│                                               │
│                                               │
│                                               │
│                                               │
└─────────────────────────────────────────────┘
```

Handouts. Prior to the meeting discuss with your Ministry Planning Team whether there should be any handouts for those in attendance and, if so, what they should be. At the first meeting it will be helpful to have at least one handout summarizing the purpose of the group, what you hope to accomplish, and the general organization of the group (when and where you will meet, number of meetings, length of each meeting, etc.).

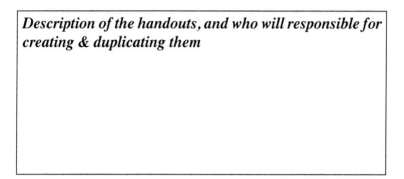

Description of the handouts, and who will responsible for creating & duplicating them

<u>Relationship building</u>. The people who are at the meeting came for a purpose (the "benefit" was worth the "risk"). At the same time, an important part of the success of your group/ministry will be to help people feel comfortable with each other and make new friends. Providing a place where people can get to know each other on a more personal basis should be a part of every meeting. In a sense, you are providing a "greenhouse" where relationships can flourish and grow.

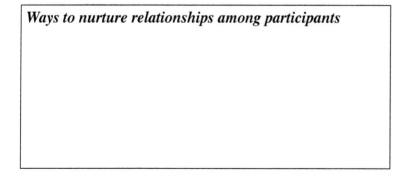

Ways to nurture relationships among participants

<u>Setting the Direction</u>. You want participants to eventually think of it as "our group" rather than "your group." Developing a sense of ownership among participants is important, but

First Place for Women
NorthRidge Church (Plymouth, MI)
A Christ-centered health program for women of all ages that incorporates Bible study, Scripture memorization, prayer and balanced eating and exercise plans. First Place provides the opportunity to change your life, not only physically but spiritually and emotionally.

requires a sensitive balance. On one hand leaders are responsible for directing the group. On the other hand, group members should also have input into the agenda and activities of the group. Always be open to, and even seek out, suggestions on the most helpful activities for the group to engage in. Just don't appear to be so disorganized that it seems you have no sense of direction for the group. Keep the overall purpose and function of the group in front of people.

How will we develop a sense of ownership among participants?

chapter thirteen

Plan for the Long-Term

Building a sense of "relational community" among those involved in your new ministry is extremely important. There will already be a natural affinity because of the common interests/concerns that brought participants together. Your goal, as a MPT, is to nurture this affinity to see this collection of people become a community of genuine, caring friends.

This chapter will give you some additional suggestions for how to nurture the relationship-growing process in Stages Two and Three of your ministry (see Chapter Ten). Remember, it will ultimately be these relationships that become the "bridges of God" for many people to come to a new Christian faith and relationship with your church family.

Heartbeat Infertility and Adoption Ministry
University Presbyterian Church (Seattle, WA)

A Christian support network for infertile couples and pre-adoptive families. Since its inception, over 160 families and professional resource people have participated in the all-volunteer ministry.

Try the Two-Step

The "two-step" means to: 1) start short, then 2) go long. It refers to the length of time the group meets. Here's how it works…

Experience shows that the best number of times for a new group to gather is between six and ten. Why? Six meetings seems to provide a minimum number of connections for people to get to know each other, develop a sense of identity, even remember other's names. The social dynamics for a collection of people to become a *group* of people seems to be five or six times together.

On the other hand, the longer you ask people to commit beyond ten gatherings before they even know each other, the less likely they will be to do so.

In your first meeting, inform participants that you will be meeting for xx weeks (somewhere between 6-10 meetings). This information on meeting length, by the way, should also have been included in your initial publicity. Explain that at the end of that period of time, the group will discuss if they want to continue meeting or disband.

In each of the six to ten meetings, spend time nurturing relationships among members and developing a sense of camaraderie in the group. Here are just a few examples of simple questions to which members could respond that will help them get to know each other and nurture a sense of empathy:

- Where would you like to go if money or time were no object?
- What is a pleasant memory from your childhood?
- What was a time you were afraid, and why?
- What is one thing that really irritates you? Makes you happy?
- Have you ever had a great idea you wonder why no one has ever come up with?
- What do you like and dislike about your job?

Perhaps have one or two people each week share their answers to these or other questions with the larger group. Or, break into smaller groups so everyone can have a part.

In the first six to ten weeks/ meetings, you will probably not see intimate friendships develop among group members. But, it is likely that people will get to know each other, remember names (be sure to use nametags at each meeting), and develop a sense of comfort and enjoy- ment in being together. Don't push relational aspects too fast, but do encourage and facilitate a growing sense of community.

Let's revisit the graphic we introduced earlier, which illus- trates the change in motivation as to why people initially begin attending a group, and then why they continue attending. (See following page.)

Parents of Special Needs Kids
Sonrise Christian Fellowship (Salt Lake City, UT)
There are unique stresses for parents of a special needs child, beginning with the day you come home with the new baby, and continuing for the rest of your life. This group provides a supportive, caring community for parents in these situations.

People decide to attend the first meeting because they believe (or hope) that the benefit will be worth the price. If they are generally happy with their first experience, they come back to the second and third meetings.

But, if you spend time in each meeting building relation- ships among those in attendance, by their third time together participants will have begun to develop a sense of famil- iarity with the people, the place, and the experience. With each subsequent meeting, assuming you continue to nurture and encourage relationships, the sense of community among members strengthens. Eventually, in the second or third month, the value of the relationships with others in the group comes to outweigh the value of the topic or focus of the group. And an amazing thing has occurred...a group has been born!

Now, for the second part of the two-step. On the next-to-last scheduled meeting, ask participants to think about what they would like to do in terms of the future of the group. Indicate that this issue will be discussed at the following (and final) meeting.

Reasons for Attending

At the final meeting, ask participants for feedback on the plusses and minuses of the group, and of past meetings. Ask the question, "What do you want to do now? We can either 1) continue meeting, or 2) stop meeting." Encourage discussion on the options. You may talk about taking a break, or finding another day or time that might be better to meet, etc.. Leave the discussion—and decision—up to the group. Explain that if the group were to decide to continue meeting, that would not mean everyone needed to continue. It could be a time where you invite new people. You may decide to review the group's purpose or activities. In opening up the destiny of the group' future to participants, you are creating a sense of ownership and identity that will be helpful for the long-term.

If you decide to keep meeting, here are some ideas on how to continue building and nurturing the sense of community among group members…

<u>Go To Special Events Together</u>. If there are activities (church-related or otherwise) that sound like fun, encourage some or all of the group members to go together. This might include:

- see a movie
- hear a special speaker related to your area of interest
- participate in a conference related to your area of interest
- go for pizza after a meeting
- attend a church- or community-sponsored event together
- work on a church- or community-sponsored service project

In these relationship-building activities, be sure that church attenders in your group don't inadvertently form "cliques" by spending all their time with each other and none with their new non-member acquaintances. If you see this happening, privately encourage the church members to involve the non-members in their social interaction. You don't want your ministry/group to become a place where the church people are the "insiders" and the unchurched people are the "outsiders."

Scuba Diving Ministry
St. Alban's Congregational Church (St. Albans, NY)
The scuba diving ministry was conceived to provide an opportunity for young African/ Caribbean/ Latin American youth to explore the sport and vocation of scuba diving.

<u>Have a Party</u>! There's always a good reason for a party. Maybe it's a birthday…a new baby…a wedding engagement…a military vet coming home…a job promotion… Or combine three or four reasons! People being honored feel esteemed, and all those celebrating feel closer to each other.

<u>Help Someone in Need</u>. Working together to help someone in need is one of the best ways to build relationships. When a need comes to your attention of someone in the group, their family, friends, or in the community, ask if they would be interested in helping out. Imagine the common and powerful bond as you work together to clean up the yard of an older widow, go shopping for school supplies with kids from a needy family, bring food to a mom and baby just home from the hospital. One of the best ways to learn about God's love is to be channels of that love to others. And even non-Christians can experience the joy in that!

<u>Appoint a Chaplain</u>. Regardless of the kind of ministry/group you have started, you should appoint someone to function as group chaplain. This person would bring a relevant devotional thought and prayer at each gathering…circulate and deliver get-well cards to anyone in the group who is sick… pray for, send flowers, or visit friends or relatives of group members in special need. The chaplain's purpose is to bring a spiritual perspective to the group and its activities.

The chaplain would also keep a record of special concerns and prayer needs of members in the group to be sure they are addressed at each meeting and not forgotten from one meeting to the next. If there is a special need or prayer request of someone in the group (or their family), the chaplain might ask whether that person would like a visit from your pastor for prayer.

As your new ministry group moves beyond a short-term topical focus to a long-term relational focus, an important "value added benefit" appears. Participants no longer focus just on their immediate felt needs, but begin to experience the joy of meeting deeper human needs in the context of real community. And the process of giving and receiving God's love continues.

Between Jobs Ministry
Northwest Bible Church
(Spring, TX)
We provide encouragement, information, networking, spiritual guidance, and job search skills training in a Christian setting. The ministry is open to jobseekers of all backgrounds.

chapter fourteen

Assess and Enlarge Your Ministry

This final step in launching a successful Heartbeat ministry will help you: 1) step back and take a look at what you've learned, and 2) step forward by increasing the number of people who will be positively affected by your new ministry.

Looking Back—Where Have We Come?
The chances are good that you have learned much since you first set out to pursue your passion through a new ministry. Here are some questions to review with your Ministry Planning Team. Be honest in your responses:

1. Has the new group/ministry come together as you had hoped?

2. What have you learned in the process of beginning your new ministry?

3. Which of the following would you like to do?
    a. move to the next stage and enlarge the influence of your new ministry
    b. keep working with the group of people who are now involved
    c. turn the ministry/group over to someone else

    d. call it quits and move on

    e. other:

If you answered "a" to question #3, the rest of this chapter if for you. It focuses on enlarging the ministry and the number of people who will be touched by it.

Looking Forward—Planning an "Entry Event'

You've had some good experiences. You've seen some lives changed. There is good reason to think that even more people could experience God's love through your ministry. So, how do we "shift into the next gear"? The answer: Put on an Entry Event.

An "Entry Event" is defined as: "A high visibility activity/ event, sponsored by the church, designed to be of interest to churched and unchurched people in your ministry's target audience." An Entry Event is a way to introduce your new ministry to more people, particularly unchurched people, in your community. Here are a few examples of successful Entry Events that churches have conducted:

Target Audience	Entry Event
Parents of adolescents	Father-Daughter Valentine's banquet
Sports enthusiasts	Super Bowl Sunday
Newlyweds	1-day conference with workshops, display booths, panel discussion, entertainment, etc.
Families in which both parents work	Family taffy pull
Single parents	Trip to a local sports game
Golfers	Golf tournament

People needing financial help	Tax planning workshop
Recent divorcees	1-day conference
New neighbors	"Welcome to the Neighborhood" day

The purpose of an "Entry Event" is to introduce your church's ministry to prospective new participants. The Entry Event should have a natural appeal to the people in your target audience, since the goal is to see a large number of these people from your target audience attend the event.

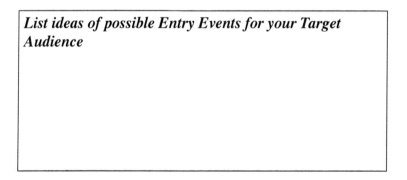

List ideas of possible Entry Events for your Target Audience

Six Steps to a Successful Entry Event

Here are a few pointers on how to have a successful Entry Event:

1. <u>Enlist people to help define, plan, and conduct the event.</u> While you may have a great idea for a high-visibility event, don't make all the decisions yourself. When others help decide what the event will be…when and where it will be held…how to promote it, they will get more involved and you will have a broader sense of ownership. Be sure to include non-members in the

planning. But the one common denominator of anyone who helps is that they have a personal interest in mission of your ministry. That is, they have the passion.

2. <u>Do a good job of publicizing the event</u>. The publicity on your Entry Event will be the first time most people in your community will have heard about your ministry. So, when you "go public," do it well and with quality. Your publicity will go a long way toward "positioning" your ministry in the minds of the people who see it.

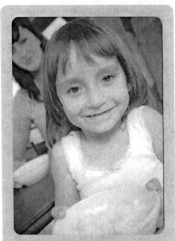

Shepherd's Pantry
Glenkirk Presbyterian Church
(Glendora, CA)

Shepherd's Pantry began in 2004 in the heart of one man at the church who wanted to provide food to those in the surrounding communities who were unable to afford it. This year we will serve over 6,000 people, with over 40 volunteers (members and non-members) helping.

3. <u>Consider holding the event in a neutral location</u>. The goal of your Entry Event is to attract a number of people who are not part of your church; or of any church. Requiring people to go to an event that is on a church campus can create a "psychological barrier" that will keep some from attending. (Would you go to an event at a Christian Science church? Or a B'hai Temple?) This doesn't mean you are trying to hide who you are or who is sponsoring the event. It means that you don't need to create artificial barriers to attending. Your goal is not to get people onto your church campus. Your goal is to establish a connection in order to begin building relationships with new people. And these relationships can happen anywhere. Possible locations, depending on what kind of event you are planning, can be a library

room, local school, community center, Elks Lodge, town hall, city park, etc..

4. The Entry Event should address a felt need which cannot be met elsewhere. The "cost-benefit" equation, which we discussed earlier, also applies to an Entry Event. This means that, in the mind of the prospective attendee, the benefit of attending event must be worth their time and effort. When you are deciding what kind of event to put on, be sure it offers enough benefit for the cost. And when you are writing the publicity, focus on those benefits—as seen through the eyes of your target audience.

5. Obtain the name and contact information of participants. The names of people who attend your Entry Event should be added to your "prospect list." These are people who likely be responsive to future invitations to your ministry's other activities. You could use registration cards for those who attend. Some churches have door prizes donated by members or community businesses, with the winners being drawn from the registration cards submitted.

Boy's Soccer League
First Assembly of God
(Ft. Myers, FL)
Every Thursday night at 6:30 p.m. in the church gym. Over 40 boys get together for great competition. Remember, you don't have to be a member of the church to join any of our sports leagues. Bring a friend or coworker.

6. Introduce your ministry at the Entry Event. The event should have a natural "next step" which people can take if they are interested in learning about other related activities or how to get involved. Extend an invitation to the next gathering of your ministry. Distribute an informative brochure with time, date, and directions to the next gath-

ering. Or, offer an opportunity to be added to the mailing list or e-mail list for announcements of future events. Make it easy for people to learn more about the ministry and take a "baby step" toward getting more involved.

Below is a list of responsibilities for planning an Entry Event. It will be helpful to put several names by each area.

PLANNING AN ENTRY EVENT

Program Planning (possible names) _____ _____

- Coordinating the overall event and its various components
- Recruiting and communicating with platform personnel

Room/Facility Set-Up (possible names) _____ _____

- Selection of where the event will be held
- Room/facility preparation
- Lighting, electrical, sound, etc.
- Refreshments & logistics

Promotion/Invitations (possible names) _____ _____

- Determining the media to be used (i.e. mailings, newspaper ads, phone calls), and how it will be designed
- Coordinating the promotion process
- Managing the advertising budget

Support Personnel (possible names)_____ _____

- Identifying "hosts" who will serve before and after the event
- Identifying other support staff that will be necessary

Evaluation & Record Keeping (possible names) _____ _____

- Evaluating the event
- Obtaining (and cataloging) names and addresses of those who attend

Other Responsibilities (possible names)_____

The Single Message

If you have identified a need, and designed and promoted the Entry Event as a genuine response to the need, you should attract a good number of people. There is one message (regardless of the kind of event you host) that you should communicate. The message is: *"There is Hope!"* *Hope* helps people face the future. Hope does not deny there will be problems. But hope means those problems can be handled. For the unchurched man or woman on the street, the idea that there may actually be a way to make sense out of a seemingly senseless life is a tantalizing idea. An Entry Event that carries a message of hope

Travel Club Ministry
Trinity Ref. Presbyterian Church (Tampa, FL)

This group meets once a month to explore our world together via documentaries, films, speakers and road trips. A light lunch is served. Travel Club is meant to build friendships, as well as to educate.

says life can be better...change can happen...a meaningful, significant, purposeful life really may be possible.

This message of "hope" may be communicated through a testimony from a church member. It may be a brief devotional from the pastor. It may be through a prayer, a panel discussion, or printed literature. It's probably not wise to give a "hard-sell" evangelistic pitch. But, do try to give participants a taste of "water where you will never thirst again."

Follow up Your Contacts

If you did a good job of getting people's names and addresses. Now follow them up. Mail a brochure and "thanks for attending" note. Invite them to a related activity. Start some new groups for new people. Expand the variety of groups and activities in your ministry. And begin planning another Entry Event.

Part Three

Bring Life to
Your Heartbeats…

chapter fifteen

Ministry Coach: Your Side-Door Contractor

I learned a long time ago that building things was not my spiritual gift! After catastrophes in my kitchen, garage, bedroom, roof, and backyard fence, I have learned that if I want a project done right, I call a contractor. My peace of mind, plus the time, money, and frustration saved, are good reasons why someone else does the job besides me. If you are a pastor considering some new side-doors in your church, I strongly recommend you take the same approach.

Chances are that while reading this book you have already thought to yourself, "A good idea, but I just don't have the time." If you have such apprehensions, my reaction is...great! In fact, I hope you feel quite overwhelmed with the prospect of personally overseeing the construction of side-doors in your church! Because you shouldn't be the one doing it. You need a contactor. You need a "Ministry Coach."

What is a Ministry Coach?

A Heartbeat Ministry Coach is your church's "contractor" for building successful side-doors. The Ministry Coach may be full-time (for a larger church) or part-time; paid or volunteer. It may be someone who is already serving the church in some capacity. And, it may actually be several people who are Ministry Coaches working in tandem.

The Coach is not the person who does the work of "building" the side-door. Rather, he/she is the one who understands the goal, knows the process, and helps others follow the blueprint of starting successful new ministries in the church. I mentioned Alan Nelson's comment earlier in this book, but let me share it again: "...every church should have someone (besides the pastor) who will champion the equipping value and develop ministry teams to implement the process."[1] He's right!

We introduced the idea of a Ministry Coach in Chapter Five with the flow chart outlining a sequence for success-fully starting a new ministry. Here I would like to revisit this chart and look specifically at the Ministry Coach's role in each step. In fact, this chapter could be considered a "job description" for an effective Ministry Coach.

What Does the Ministry Coach do?

Prerequisites: The Pastor and Ministry Coach must have a relationship of confidence, respect, and trust. If the Pastor is going to delegate authority to the Coach, then he/she must have assurance that the creation of the new ministries in the church is in good hands.

In addition to being trusted by the pastor and other church leaders, the Ministry Coach should:

- be committed to the church's philosophy of lay ministry and outreach;
- be able to genuinely encourage people, while at the same time hold them accountable to goals, budgets and deadlines;
- have the spiritual gift of administration.

Job Description: The role and responsibility of a Ministry Coach can be organized into three main categories:

I.   IDENTIFY passion and potential for new ministries in the church.
II. SUPPORT those people involved in pursuing their passion.
III. COMMUNICATE with pastor, other church leaders, and the Ministry Planning Team so that everyone is informed and supportive of the new endeavor.

Let's examine each of these three areas...

I. IDENTIFY

The Ministry Coach's first and ongoing task is to let people in the congregation know that it's OK to dream about a new ministry. In fact, it's OK to do more than just dream, it's OK to pursue that dream and know that the church will help them do so! "We try to find out what our church members enjoy doing, apart from attending worship and going to Bible study," says Todd Pridemoor, Minister of Outreach at Memorial Bible Church in Columbia, Missouri. "We encourage people to think outside the box. There is almost no activity that is so secular that it cannot be used to create a side-door into the congregation."[2]

The flow chart below was introduced in Chapter Five. It shows the sequence of starting a new ministry. We discussed each step in this process. Now let's look specifically at Steps 1 & 4, and how the Ministry Coach can help create a "ministry greenhouse" where members' "passion seeds" can grow into healthy living ministries.

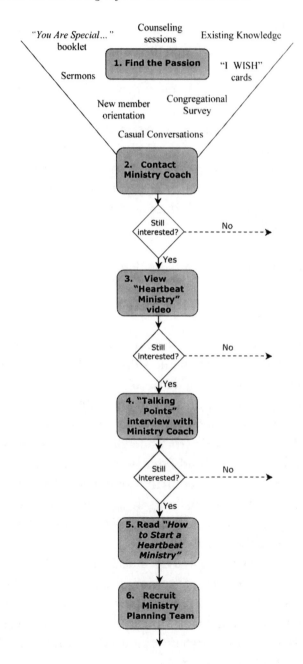

Find the Passion

We have already discussed how to identify passions of members which might grow into a ministry. Here are some ways the Ministry Coach can facilitate this "passion prospecting"...

✓ Teach about the importance of finding a ministry—or creating one—in the new members' class.

✓ Print and place "I WISH" cards on information tables, in visitor packets, in pew backs, brochure racks...and then mentioned them regularly.

✓ Distribute the "You Are Special..." booklets whenever and wherever appropriate (see Appendix D).

✓ Encourage the pastor to preach a series of messages on lay ministry and each member's unique part in the body of Christ.

✓ Conduct a Congregational Survey to identify interests and passions in the church (see Appendix A).

✓ Use the church newsletter and worship service to highlight new ministry initiatives that members are already taking.

✓ Ask small group leaders and class teachers to listen for interests, needs, or experiences in people's lives that might be the basis of a Heartbeat ministry, and then send any ideas on to the Ministry Coach.

✓ Give copies of the "Do You Have a Heartbeat?" CD to people in the church who might have an interest in starting a new ministry. The video may be viewed or downloaded from www.HeartbeatMinistries.net, or seen on U-Tube (search: "Heartbeat Ministry video").

✓ Hold periodic "New Ministry Conversations" after church. These are 15-20 minute open-ended brainstorming sessions held periodically after church to explore whether there are enough people with an interest in a particular area to explore a Heartbeat ministry. Each ministry conversation meeting should focus on just one topic, which would grow out of your analysis of the Congregational Survey. A "New Ministry Conversation" could also be called by someone in the church related to a particular need they have seen in the community.

Conduct "Talking Points" Interviews

As a culture of "ministry birthing" grows in your church, and people begin to think about possible ministries related to their interests, an increasing number of people will want to talk with someone about it. One of the tasks of the Ministry Coach is to be that person. The "Talking Points" interview (#4 in the flowchart) is where people can explore their dreams of new ministries. (See Appendix B for the Talking Points interview questions.)

Prior to the interview, the church member with the ministry dream should have read the *"You Are Special..."* booklet (see Appendix D) and viewed the 10-minute "Do You Have a Heartbeat?" video (at www.HeartbeatMinistires.net). Interviewees should write out their answers to the "Talking Points" questions and bring two copies to the interview.

The "Talking Points" conversation is not unlike a job interview. The person will be representing your church and be a part of your public image in the community. So, be careful in this initial screening discussion. It can often be helpful to invite another person to sit in on the meeting and then debrief later. (A third person is particularly important if the Ministry Coach and interviewee are of opposite gender.)

As in a job interview, look for how the person dresses and communicates...was he on time...is she enthusiastic about the new ministry idea...could they actually make it happen. The instructions in the "Talking Points" discussion guide says: "Prior to the meeting please think about, and then write out, your responses to the questions below." Did the person follow these directions?

If the person is not well-known among church leaders, the Ministry Coach should solicit input from others in the church who know him. What kind of track record does he have with previous responsibilities in the church? If she recently transferred from another church, what does her previous pastor say about her?

An essential part of a Heartbeat ministry is outreach to non-members. Does he have a desire to reach out to unchurched people, or does he seem to prefer focusing on "our people" in the church?

In the interview, tell the person that it is the policy of the church to run a background check on all those who represent the church. Ask if she is OK with that. (A good source for background checks is GROUP Publishing, www.Group.com).

The final item of the "Talking Points" discussion guide is to make a list of "next steps" to take after the meeting. If there is a lack of clarity about giving the church member a green light to proceed, a second meeting should be scheduled several weeks later. Give the interviewee a few assignments, such as talking with others who might be interested in helping with the new ministry. Encourage the person to bring some of those interested people to the next meeting.

While there may some questions about the qualifications or leadership skills of the person, be sure not to underestimate the power of enthusiasm and vision. There are many exceptional Heartbeat ministries in churches today that began with a person who had little experience or charismatic leadership. But she believed so strongly in her vision, and pursued it with such enthusiasm, that she became the spark that started a new ministry and side-door into the church.

In the "Talking Point" interviews don't feel that every person must be given a go-ahead. While there is nothing better than an enthusiastic person passionately pursuing a new ministry, there can be nothing worse than a misguided or wrongly motivated individual making public missteps in the name of your church. I am reminded of my father's advice in my younger courting days: "Marry in haste...repent at leisure." He was telling me to be sure I was picking the right person going into a long commitment. I would give you the same advice. As a church leader, you are not required to give anyone who approaches you the authority to act under the auspices of the church. Not only are you putting the church's name and reputation on the line, but you should be considering the church's legal liability, as well. Be in contact with your church's attorney anytime you have a question regarding possible liability issues. In other words, you need to have confidence in the people who will be representing your church.

If there is consensus that both the idea and the person are winners, the interviewee should be given a copy of the *How to Start a Heartbeat Ministry* manual.[3] Go over it together and point out the importance of following the sequence. The person should first read through the entire workbook, and then focus on the first step: Identify a Ministry Planning Team and a Prayer Support Team. Once the Ministry Planning Team has been assembled, a meeting with the Ministry Coach should be scheduled to review the next steps and reaffirm the church's support for this upcoming venture.

II. SUPPORT

In addition to continuously "prospecting" for passion among members, a second responsibility of the Ministry Coach is to encourage and help those who are pursuing their passion in a new ministry. Just as a newborn needs special attention in the first months, the people nursing the new vision need that same special attention and support.

The First Crucial Months

It will be uncharted territory for the Ministry Planning Team (MPT) as they set out in pursuit of their dream. It is to everyone's advantage for the Ministry Coach and the MPT to stay in close communication in the early stages of the journey. The Ministry Coach should not wait for the leader to call but be proactive in contacting him/her. The "next steps" that were part of the "Talking Points" interview should be regularly checked and reviewed with the leader.

The Ministry Coach should conduct research on the topic of the new ministry, and pass along websites, churches with similar ministries, books, organizations, and other helpful resources to the Team leader. If a person (in or outside the church) is identified who has experience that could be helpful, the name should be sent to the MPT leader for follow up.

It is a supportive gesture for the church to provide funds for the Ministry Planning Team to attend a related training conference. My wife is currently beginning a Heartbeat ministry in our church for families of children with special needs. Our church paid for her MPT to attend a Joni & Friends Conference nearby. The Team was greatly encouraged by the church's support of their new initiative, and the conference gave them new ideas to improve their fledgling ministry.

The Ministry Coach should create an electronic or physical file for all information related to each new ministry. Copies of e-mails to and from group leaders should be kept. Any comments, questions, or concerns following phone conversations should be noted. This information will be important in reports to the pastor and church leadership, and will be useful reference if any complications develop. In other words, create a paper trail.

The Ministry Planning Team and the Prayer Support Team should be publicly affirmed for their vision and commitment. In so doing, those involved will be affirmed, and others in the church will be encouraged to reflect on their own passions and possibilities.

Three Important Priorities...

In my research, I have seen three critical areas where new ministries can get off-course. As part of the support role, the Ministry Coach should keep these key issues in front of the every Ministry Planning Team. Like a three-legged stool, if one leg is removed the stool comes crashing down. These three issues are critical for a new ministry to become a successful side-door into your church. So, it is easier to address them early rather than try to fix them later.

1. Outward-Focused

When church people organize special activities and start new groups, they have a tendency to recruit participants from within their own church. Don't let the MPTs make this mistake! The planning teams should give much attention and effort to connecting with unchurched people—from the outset. A new ministry that is comprised of only churched participants will set an inward-focused precedent that will be very difficult to change. Of course, there will be some in the church who have an interest and will want to participate in the new ministry. And, they should be encouraged to do so. But the team's planning and programming of the new ministry should assume that non-members will be at the first and all subsequent gatherings. The Ministry Coach should keep this outward-focused thinking in front of every new ministry planning team, and regularly ask how they are doing at including non-members in their activities. Accountability in this area is important or the priority of involving non-members will slip through the cracks. And if it does, the "side-door" will close!

In addition to unchurched people, three other "people groups" should be invited to the ministry's initial (and all subsequent) activities: 1) recent church visitors, 2) new church members, and 3) less active or inactive church members. Newcomers (visitors or new members) are still on the relational fringes of the church's social network and are hoping to make new friends. Involvement in new ministries can be the perfect solution—it provides the new ministry with enthusiastic participants, and it helps newcomers make friends and connections around common interests. Of course, not every new church attender or member will be interested in the new ministry. But the Ministry Coach should give the names and contact information of all recent church visitors, new attenders, and new members to the MPT who should then invite these newcomers to their events.

Concerning inactive members, we know that drop-outs do not generally return to the "same church" they left. But a new ministry initiative, particularly if it focuses on a person's strongly held need or interest, can be a good reason for some inactives to try the church again. It may well begin their journey toward reconciliation with lost friends and the Christian community. It never hurts to invite them.

2. *Spiritual Exposure*

A second place where side-doors can get off-track is if the group does not develop an effective spiritual dynamic. "The most significant thing to consider is what can be done so that those unchurched people who have entered your side door will have the opportunity to experience and respond to God as they feel led to do so," observes Todd Pridemore, an architect of many side-doors in his church.[4] The new ministry is not just a class on car repair, or a group for craft-making. While repairing cars or making crafts can be excellent reasons for like-minded people to get together, the Ministry

Planning Team should understand that these activities are not the ultimate reason for the new ministry.

Every gathering of the new ministry should provide an opportunity for participants to have some exposure to God, and God's people. For example, a Baptist church in Riverside, California began a children's photography group as a new Heartbeat ministry. The idea was conceived by a professional photographer in the church. Twice a month on Saturday mornings the parents and kids gather at the church for a lesson on cameras and photography. Each child receives a throw-away camera and then the group leaves on a field trip to practice their new photography skills. But before they leave, the leader gives a short talk about capturing the beauty of God's creation and how God's special fingerprint can be seen and photographed if they look closely for it. Then one of the children from the church prays for God's protection before they depart.[5]

Another example of building a spiritual dynamic into a Heartbeat ministry is Pump-N-Praise, a women's aerobics group at Wheaton Bible Church that was started by two young moms. Pump-N-Praise is "...a 50-minute aerobic exercise program suited for women of most abilities and choreographed to contemporary Christian music. From warm-up to cool down, listen to positive, life-affirming words to strengthen your spirit while you stretch, dance and tone up your body. Share prayer requests and praises at the end of each class as we exercise the power of prayer."[6]

The Glendora Church of the Brethren began a Heartbeat ministry when several church members were given permission to dig up part of the church's side yard and turn it into a garden. Members in the community were invited to join in and get dirty. Six months later, at their first "eat-in", the pastor led the group in prayer before the 30 gardeners (two-thirds of whom were not members) enjoyed eating the fruits of their labors.

Effective disciple-making provides multiple Christian exposures. A research study at the University of Illinois compared people who came to Christian faith and became active in a church, against others who made a Christian decision but did not become actively involved. The "variable" was the number of exposures both groups had to the Christian message *before* their faith commitment. Those who became active in a church following their conversion had been exposed to the Christian message over *six* different times and ways before their decision. Those who did not become involved averaged only *two* Christian exposures prior to their decision. The researcher concluded that those who had multiple Christian contacts had a far better understanding of what their commitment really involved.[7] So, if your goal is disciple-making, and not just decision-making, provide many different opportunities for non-believers to see and hear what it means to be a Christ-follower. If/when they decide to follow him, the chances go up dramatically that they will be active in your church for many years to come.

3. Nurturing Relationships

A third priority for every Heartbeat ministry, and one where I find some groups stumble, is in the process of intentionally creating and nurturing deeper relationships among participants. Relationships are the "glue" that keep people coming back.

A doctoral dissertation compared the number of close friends that active church members had made in the year following their church affiliation, and then compared that to the number of friends church drop-outs had made in their first year. The study found those who remained active in their church had made an average of seven "good friends;" those who left the church had made less than two.[8]

The growth of relationships in a group has been studied by specialists for many years. Mark Knapp and Anita

Vangelisti[9] suggest that relationships among group members go through certain stages from first meeting to deep intimacy. Not all relationships, obviously, grow to the most intimate level. But understanding relational development can be helpful for Ministry Coach and ministry leader.

The first stage in Knapp & Vangelisti's model is the *initiating* stage. This is when people first meet each other and assess the compatibility and comfort they feel with the others. At this point, people work very hard to present themselves as likeable and interesting. They tend to select their words carefully and are reserved in their exposure of more personal issues.

The second stage is the *experimenting* stage. Here individuals ask questions in order to gain information and attempt to reduce their uncertainty about one another. In this stage most individuals expect the others in the group to be upbeat and positive (not morose and depressed), to exhibit appropriate dress and hygiene, and to be courteous (not boorish). If not enough persons in the group meet those expectations, others will often decide not to spend anymore time participating.

Assuming a sense of comfort and trust has begun to develop among group members, and they pass the initial tests, members move on to the *intensifying* stage. In this stage, they disclose increasingly personal information about themselves. The group develops routines, identity, jargon, and traditions. Members often use the word "we" to describe the group. Conversations have fewer formalities and are often continued from previous meetings. Greater empathy develops among group members as the concern of one becomes the concern of the whole.

The fourth stage is called the *integrating* stage. This is when participants' identity becomes, in part, associated with the group; they think of themselves as members of the group. Participants come to value how much they share in common—attitudes, interests, concerns. The group, and individual members, spend discretionary time together. It also becomes increasingly difficult for a newcomer to break into the social dynamics of the group unless he/she is a close friend or relative of someone already in the group.

So, the development of relationships in the new ministry is quite important. The Ministry Coach should encourage the leaders to include activities that intentionally nurture and grow relationships. In an ideal situation, participants will experience a change over time in why they actually attend the gathering. The motivation will move from learning about a topic or participating in an activity, to spending time with friends and feeling valued and loved. When that transition occurs, members' commitment to the group becomes substantially stronger, and their participation becomes an increasingly important part of their life.

Leader Training

As Heartbeat ministries begin to develop in your church, Heartbeat leaders should be gathered together at least once a quarter for communication, updates, and review. During these meetings focus on one or more of six characteristics of a healthy group:

- *Spiritual growth*—God's love, when experienced, is irresistible
- *Service opportunities*—learning from Christ means learning to give
- *Outreach to others*—in the long run, eternity is a long time
- *Meaningful friendships*—few people these days get to experience the joy of being accepted and loved for who they are
- *Intellectual growth*—faith does not mean we don't grow in our understanding

- *Fellowship/fun*—nothing like just having a good old time together

Encourage Heartbeat ministry leaders to integrate each of these six aspects into their annual planning. While each component does not need to be included in each meeting, these six "waypoints" should be the basis for navigating the long-term journey of every Heartbeat ministry.

The quarterly gatherings can also focus on other topics of interest to Heartbeat leaders, such as:

- Ways to build a caring community
- How to provide Christian contacts and exposures
- The role of the group chaplain
- Upcoming church events to which others can be invited
- Successes and challenges of starting a new ministry
- Qualities of strong friendships and how to nurture them
- Keeping an outward-focus in the ministry
- Ways of growing your ministry
- Planning "Entry Events"

III. COMMUNICATE

We have looked at two general areas of responsibility for the Ministry Coach: "Identifying" passions in the church, and "Supporting" those who are taking the bold step of starting a new ministry. The third area is equally important—"Communicating" with key people in the church.

Most marriage counselors agree that communication is the key to a successful relationship. It is also a key to a successful side-door strategy in your church. Here are two important aspects of the Ministry Coach's communication responsibilities:

Communicate with the Pastor

A monthly face-to-face update with the pastor should include:

- Ways that members have been encouraged to consider a "Heartbeat Ministry" in the past month.
- The number of "Talking Point" interviews conducted, and with whom (see Appendix B).
- Progress of each Heartbeat ministry, including:
    o Effectiveness of the Ministry Planning Teams
    o Number of meetings and activities of each new ministry
    o Number of people involved (members and non-members)
    o Trends and momentum of each ministry
    o Future plans of each ministry
- General needs/concerns regarding your church's side-door ministry strategy

Communicate with Church Leaders

The Ministry Coach should encourage other church leaders to be sensitive to any major events going on in the lives of the members with whom they come in contact. Events such as an unexpected medical or financial condition, a new family member, or a new hobby can often be the seeds for a new side-door ministry with just a little encouragement. Remember, God doesn't waste experience. If any such situations come to the attention of a church leader, he/she should pass along the name and situation to the Ministry Coach.

Another communication responsibility for the Ministry Coach is when a new ministry initiative is being considered. Organizational structures, boards, and committees in the church should be informed earlier rather than later. However, Lyle Schaller makes an interesting recommenda-

tion as to how the new Heartbeat ministry should be introduced to a church board. He says to present the idea "...
as an announcement rather than a request. Then follow the
announcement with: 'unless, of course, the board objects'."[10]

If a new Heartbeat ministry looks like it might affect an
existing ministry area in the church, it is wise for the Ministry
Coach to connect with the church leaders who work in that
area. For example, if someone has come forward with the
dream of starting an after-school homework club, this could
affect the children's ministry in the church. Set up a meeting
with all those involved to discuss and share dreams. Ask for
suggestions from the "powers that be," on how to support
and even cooperate with the new initiative. Another purpose
behind these gatherings is to create allies earlier rather than
ignore these people and create adversaries later.

Prevent Problems Before They Become Problems

Problems have a way of demoralizing enthusiasm, especially in the early weeks and months of a new ministry. The
more experience the Ministry Coach has, the more these
problems can be anticipated and addressed before they
become debilitating. In the following chapter we will look
at how the Ministry Coach can spend a little time preventing
problems rather than a lot of time reacting to them...

chapter sixteen

"If Only a Map Existed..."

A n article recently appeared in a online newspaper, the headline reading: "If only a map existed..."[1] Egypt, it turns out, is the second most heavily mined country in the world (after Afghanistan), due to the deadly legacy of WWII German general Erwin Rommel. Allied troops battled Rommel throughout North Africa between 1940 – 1943. In his retreat, Rommel left millions of landmines beneath the sandy surface, waiting to cause havoc. Besides the 8,000 lives that have been lost, the mines now make inaccessible natural resources of nearly a billion cubic meters of underground water, 4.8 million barrels of oil, 13 trillion cubic feet of natural gas. But only 3 million of the estimated 20 million mines have been found and cleared. Referring to the dramatic potential development of the country that might occur if these resources could be tapped, the Egyptian president recently lamented, "If only a map existed to show us the mines..."

When you harness the "natural resources" of interests, experiences, and passions in your church, you will be tapping into a powerful development tool for new ministry and outreach. But there are "land mines" that can frustrate your best intentions if you aren't careful. In this chapter I would like to share with you a "map" of some of the most dangerous potential problems you might encounter as you start on your journey of building side-door ministries. This map will help you to avoid some of the "land mines" that can keep you from tapping the rich human resources God has put just beneath the surface in your church.

THE MINES and THE MAP

LAND MINE #1: **A person in your church wants to start a Heartbeat ministry, but you know little about him/her.**

If you are in a church of several hundred people or more, there will probably (and hopefully) be some who are interested in starting a Heartbeat ministry who have not had a previous role in church leadership. This, of course, is no reason to discourage the person from reflecting on their heartbeat and considering a new ministry through the church. Every current leader in your church was new and untested at one time.

In this case, consider looking for a co-leader of the proposed Heartbeat ministry who has both the leadership experience and a passion for the ministry. Shared leadership can be a very positive dynamic in any case, assuming the two personalities are compatible. It halves the load and doubles the power. In fact, it's a reasonable idea to explore co-leadership with anyone who comes to you with a vision for a new ministry.

We mentioned the value of doing some research on the person before the "Talking Points" interview. Check with the leader of any class or small group in which the person participates. Run a background check. Go online to see if the person has an account on a social networking site, and see what you can learn about him/her. (Type in "social networking websites" on Wikipedia for an extensive list.) Remember, every Heartbeat ministry will be a church-sponsored activity with all the liability that goes along with it. You need to be confident in the people who will be representing your church.

I was talking recently with Brian Uyeda, director of lay ministry at Saddleback Church. The congregation has over 20,000 people on an average weekend, with over 60% involved in ministry at some time during the year. Many of these ministries grow out of members' passions. I asked Bryan how the church avoids putting the wrong people in the wrong place. "We can tell pretty quickly in our first meeting whether we're likely to have problems," he said. "We usually have several of our staff in the meeting and later compare notes." Whether you are in a church of 20,000 or 20, be diligent in screening your future representatives. Remember that a Heartbeat ministry will come in contact with a number of unchurched people in your community. You want those contacts to be positive.

LAND MINE #2: You're skeptical that the person with the Heartbeat idea has the necessary leadership or initiative.

Not everyone has the leadership ability, administrative wherewithal, or even the social skills to turn a heartbeat dream into a heartbeat reality. But then, not every part of the body can throw a rock, or smell a rose, or hear a spoken word. So, what do you do when you have an enthusiastic visionary, but your intuition or experience tells you it's not likely to come together under his/her direction.

Ask the following three questions:

1. *"Does the heartbeat idea, itself, have merit?"* If the answer is "no," then you have both the wrong idea and the wrong person and should gracefully move on. If your answer is "yes, the idea does seem to have potential," ask the next question...
2. *"Are you certain of your assessment about the person?"* Don't be too quick to write off the person's ability to get things done. There's something a little different about

starting a Heartbeat ministry. It taps into a person's passion, which is not always the case in traditional lay ministry. The person may not have done very well on a previous task, but it might also be that he/she was not very motivated, gifted, or knowledgeable in that area. However, if you've been honest with yourself and still feel that the person lacks the skills to get the new ministry off the ground, go to the third question...

3. *"Is there someone in the church who might also have an interest that could fill the leadership void?"* As in the prior situation, consider the possibility of co-leaders. In fact, there is a good chance the visionary will be quite happy to even surrender the leadership responsibilities to someone more likely to see the dream realized. Most of us don't like doing what we know we're not very good at doing. So, don't assume that the person with the heartbeat idea feels they have to be in charge. Hopefully, passion is more important than power.

If you end up needing to answer question #3 before you go on, use the "Talking Points" Discussion Guide to list the "next step" with the person of finding a leader. The goal is to find a person(s) in the church willing to oversee the new ministry in the start-up phase. Rick Warren shares his church's approach to this dilemma: "Sometimes a person will have a great idea for ministry but personally doesn't have the leadership skills to pull it off. In that case, it's important to pray that God will raise up a leader who can take the ball and run with it. But if you spend all your time telling people what won't work, they'll eventually stop trying altogether."[2] If your church has a spiritual gifts discovery process, start your search with people whom the Holy Spirit has gifted in leadership. There may be a person in your church with the gift of leadership but nowhere to use her gift. This might be a match made in heaven: a Heartbeat visionary with a passion but lacking the gift of leadership, together with a gifted leader in your church without a place to use her gift! If the prospective leader has an interest, schedule a follow-up meeting with you, the heartbeat visionary and the prospective leader.

If a potential leader cannot be identified, you and the heartbeat visionary should agree to put the idea on hold until a leader is forthcoming. Think twice (even three times) about giving a green light to someone who will have leadership and/or organizational challenges down the road. I can't say it too often: they will be representing your church.

LAND MINE #3: **The visionary can't get a Ministry Planning Team organized.**

After the "Talking Points" interview, the first step will be for the visionary to recruit: 1) a Ministry Planning Team and 2) a Prayer Support Team (see Chapter Six). The benefits of a team are:

- It's more fun going on a journey with others who share the excitement.
- It's nice to have people to encourage each other when it's needed.
- It's easier to come up with good ideas together than alone.
- It's just a more effective and efficient way to get things done.

It shouldn't be hard for the visionary to find people who agree to pray for the endeavor. (So, who's going to say, "No, I won't pray for you"?!) But recruiting a Ministry Planning Team of people who agree to spend the next year meeting, planning, and working on a particular project will be more challenging. Serving on such a team will require a commitment of time and effort that not everyone will be ready to make. But remember the recommendation to the lay leader in Chapter Six: "A Ministry Planning Team is so important to the success of your new venture that if you can't find at least two other people to help you get started on this first stage of the journey, you should *not* continue until you find some."

There may be different reasons why a visionary has trouble recruiting a team:

Reason #1: The visionary doesn't have the contacts.
Reason #2: The vision isn't compelling.
Reason #3: No one wants to work with the person.

Here are a few thoughts on each:

Reason #1: In the *How to Start a Heartbeat Ministry* guide, the suggestion is made to the leader to look for Ministry Planning Team members among: a) friends and relatives, b) people who are also passionate about the same issue. However, if you are a church of over 200 people, chances are good that not everyone knows each other well enough to know their passions, interests, and concerns. In this case the Ministry Coach should help in the process of bringing people together who have a similar heartbeat interest. Other church staff or leaders may know of members who might be interested in the proposed ministry. A notice can be placed in the bulletin or an announcement made during the worship service, such as: "There has been discussion recently about the possibility of our church beginning a new ministry in the area of —. If you have an interest and would like to share your thoughts, there will be a short 20-minute meeting after the service in the —."

Also, remember that not every member of the Ministry Planning Team must be a church member. In fact, it may be beneficial if one or two people on the Planning Team are *not* involved in the church. Lyle Schaller agrees: "Enlist volunteers who will help create multiple entry paths for new people. Include prospective people in these efforts. Most prospective members prefer to help pioneer the new ventures rather than join the old."[3] Involving non-members will "freshen up" the group and bring new ideas for getting things done. One thing it will certainly do—build friendships between members and non-members who are serving together on the Planning Team. With this approach, you will begin to achieve one of your goals—building relationships—even before the new ministry begins.

Reason #2: The visionary may have trouble recruiting a MPT because the vision, or at least their communication of the vision, is not compelling. To deal with this before it is a problem, help the person clarify the answer to the question: "What would this ministry look like five years from today?" The Ministry Coach should dream with the visionary about the possibilities of this ministry if it lived up to God's expectations. Communicating a vision of "the promised land" is the best way to enlist people to begin a heartbeat journey. When the visionary can see, feel, and touch this dream, then sharing it with others who may already have an interest in the topic will make the vision much more compelling.

On the other hand, the person may be having trouble finding people who catch the vision because no one else has that same passion. This doesn't necessarily mean the vision should be abandoned. Sometimes it takes a "vision-pioneer" to tenaciously call people to a place beyond their current condition. A church in Snellville, Georgia has a wonderful Cancer Care ministry today that grew out of just one woman's initial passion and commitment. No one else had come forward with the idea, but when this woman was given a forum to voice her passion—and the human need such a ministry would touch—she had no trouble finding volunteers.

If the visionary cannot recruit a MPT, but you decide to encourage the person to move ahead with his/her passion anyway, the Ministry Coach will most likely be required to spend considerably more time guiding and helping in the start-up of this particular ministry. And the odds of the new ministry being successful go down significantly.

Reason #3. If you suspect a problem with the interpersonal skills of the visionary, and it seems to be confirmed by the person's inability to recruit a MPT, face the fact that it is probably time to cut bait. (That's a fishing expression I learned from my Minnesota brother-in-law. I believe it means, "pack it up and call it a day.") It may well be God's way of saying, "not now."

LAND MINE #4: **The Ministry Planning Team runs out of gas before getting off the ground.**

This problem is usually the result of Planning Team members lacking a clear sense of direction and/or making any significant progress. The *How to Start a Heartbeat Ministry* workbook provides specific steps for starting a new ministry. If the leader and MPT follow the sequence and timeline they should make good progress. Encourage the leader to avoid letting the group get too creative "doing their own thing," and to follow the *Heartbeat* planning guide as much as possible. Check to see what steps they have followed in the manual, and perhaps what steps they have skipped.

Keep in regular communication with the leader of the MPT. As the Team is progressing through the *Heartbeat* manual, there are several places where the leader is asked to meet with the Ministry Coach: when she has identified her Prayer Team and Ministry Planning Team, and when she has completed the planning process for the new ministry.

Depending on the Team, you may decide to have more frequent meetings or briefings on their progress.

LAND MINE #5: **The first public meeting of the new ministry is a bust.**

If the attendance at the first gathering of the new ministry is one that everyone would prefer to forget, it is due to one of two reasons:

1. People didn't know about the meeting.
2. People did know about the meeting.

If they didn't know about it, the problem was publicity. There is a helpful chapter in the *Heartbeat* planning manual on publicity. If the MPT followed the guidelines for promoting the event the chances are good that people knew about it. However, even professional marketing agencies are constantly trying to learn how to do their job better. So, review the activities that went into advertising this first event. What about the wording of the communication...the method of invitation...the timing...the exposure to the target audience? Look at how much effort the Team put into mass invitations, compared to personal invitations (which are far more effective).

If people in the target audience *did* know about the event, the problem was not publicity, but perceived value. Those who knew about the event and chose not to attend were saying—by their absence—that the hassle of going was not worth the benefit they expected to get out of it. The risk was not worth the reward. But don't be discouraged about no-shows. Be stimulated to figure out why people didn't come if they knew about it. The Team needs to go back and ask: "Are we sure we presented the benefit of this event from the perspective of the target group?...or did we present it from what we *thought* was their perspective?" As church folks, we often presume we know how unchurched people think, feel and act. So we develop our outreach and promotion plans based on this perception. More often than not we really don't understand how people in our target group are thinking—what their "hot buttons" are that motivate them to act. We don't know how to extend an invitation that "sells the sizzle" and makes the promise worth the price. That is why the *Heartbeat* planning guide recommends the MPT conduct several focus groups to "get into the head" of their target group and find out what they really are thinking. If you spent a lot of time and money on an unattended event, and you didn't do any focus groups with your target audience, the cause for the failure may be looking at you in the mirror.

But, whatever the reason, if the first meeting was a bomb, the question is: "Now what?"

Gather the Planning Team together for a debriefing. Begin with prayer and be honest before God in expressing your feelings and desires. Then use the following questions to guide your discussion:

A. Was the disappointing turn-out a publicity problem or a perceived value problem?

B. Should we try the event again? If so, what will we do differently? How certain are we that the next time will be different?

C. If the problem was one of perceived value, we must have mis-read our target audience. How can we be sure we understand the real issues our target group is facing? Ask the question that Prince of Peace Church in Illinois asks the prospective attendees of their new groups: "What kind of group would you change your schedule to be a part of?"

D. Did we (or should we) conduct more "focus groups" to be sure we really understand the mindset of our target audience? Businesses and marketing companies often do this when it appears their marketing strategy needs to go back to the drawing board.

If the group decides to try again, it is important that they put their best effort into it. If the second attempt is also a bomb, the ministry dream is, for all practical purposes, dead.

LAND MINE #6: **Subsequent gatherings of the new ministry are going downhill in attendance and/or involvement.**

People vote with their feet. If fewer and fewer people are attending the gatherings, it is likely that the benefit is less than the cost. One nice thing about a new group or activity is that it can handle rapid change. Here are some suggestions to adjust the rudder if people don't seem to like where the boat is going:

- Be sure prospective participants know about upcoming gatherings. Don't just pass out a monthly calendar with time and dates and then hope people remember. Send e-mails. Make phone calls. Send post cards. Redundancy is the most reliable form of communication. Redundancy is the most reliable form of communication.
- Sometimes the "back door" of a group or activity can be closed simply by letting people know they were missed when they're gone. If someone misses a meeting, send them a card or an e-mail to tell them how valued they are and remind them of the time and date of the next gathering.
- Conduct an assessment of the new ministry's activities to date. Ask for input from people who have participated in one or more of the events. Include those who came initially but then stopped coming. If momentum is declining, try to answer these questions:

o *Did we clearly and specifically define our target audience?* Remember, the more specific the definition of your target audience, the more likely their interests/needs can be identified and addressed. In contrast, a broad and general description of the target audience makes it nearly impossible to provide for the needs of everyone in the group.

o *Have we accurately identified the most significant felt needs of our target audience?* It's not what *we think* is important, it's what *they feel* is important.

o *Did we focus on, and meet, those felt needs?* There are three needs that an effective Heartbeat ministry should meet (and in this order): 1) felt needs, 2) deeper needs, 3) eternal needs. But, if the first is not initially met, people won't be around for you to meet the second or third.

o *Has there been enough time and experience to conclude that there actually is a declining trend, and a change is necessary?* No ministry will see every visitor who attends come back. (You can apply the same formula for Visitor Volume and Visitor Retention that we learned earlier.) Be sure you are seeing a clear trend of an unacceptable return rate, and not just normal attrition. It is common to see declining attendance for the first 3-4 meetings and then attendance pick up after that. Because of this, you will need to start out with a large enough "critical mass" to weather this decline. Which is why it's nice to do the promotion right the first time.

- Send a survey, cover letter, and stamped return envelope to those who attended at least one gathering but did not get involved. Here is a sample survey for a support-oriented ministry that focuses on a particular problem or challenge. If the new ministry is recreationally-oriented, replace "helpful" with "enjoyable."

Our goal in the new **xxxx** group is to connect people with a common interest in: **yyyy**. We've had several gatherings over the past few months, and learned much in the process. We are now wanting to see this group move to the next level and make it even more helpful to those who are involved. Would you please take a moment to answer a few questions that will help us plan for the future. Thank you. (Note the enclosed, stamped envelope. Providing your name for Question #4 is optional.)

1. How many events of the **xxxx** ministry have you attended? _____

2. Did you find them to be helpful? (Please circle your response)
   Very much   Mostly   A little   Not at all

3. What would you suggest to make the time together more helpful?

4. If you would be interested in contributing your time and ideas to help make this group even better, please give your name and contact information below and we'll be in touch.

- Is there "ownership" of the group, or do the activities come across as an "entertainer-audience" relationship? The best way to develop commitment to a group is for participants to have a part in the group's direction. When you ask attendees to help plan future meetings/activities, you will not only improve the quality of the gatherings, you will have more people concerned with increasing the attendance. Enlarge the number of people who call it "our group" by enlarging the number who have a stake in its success.

- Here are other reasons that may be related to poor or declining participation that you and the MPT should consider...
  - o Irrelevant content
  - o Inconvenient meeting day, time, or location
  - o Length of meeting (too long or too short)
  - o Lack of (or poor) child care
  - o Unclear goals, direction, progress
  - o Inadequate leadership or facilitation
  - o Other:

LAND MINE #7: **The group/activity does not have any unchurched participants.**

This situation needs immediate attention if it continues for more than three meetings. It will be increasingly difficult to see unchurched people involved the longer the group goes on without them. Research and experience clearly show that groups have a "saturation point" that, once it is reached, make it nearly impossible for newcomers to sociologically "get in." Involving unchurched people in the Heartbeat ministry is so important that if the gathering does not have at least 25% non-members involved after the first 3 – 4 meetings, I suggest that further meetings should be suspended until a plan is developed to address the problem.

Why might there be no unchurched people involved? Here are the most likely reasons:

- They weren't *personally* invited. Personal invitations are far more effective than mass invitations, particularly for people who have no prior contact with your church. Positive responses to personal invitations from an acquaintance (i.e., e-mail, phone call, face-to-face invitation, etc.) will be approximately 28%. Responses to mass media invitations (i.e., bulk mailings, newspaper ads, posters, etc.) will be 1%, at best.

- They see the group as "too churchy." While you're not trying to hide who you are, you should be initially focusing on the common denominator that every prospective participant has in common. And it is *not* church. Remember, meet the felt needs first. Longer-term needs and eternal needs will be addressed as relationships develop.

- They are reticent to meet at a church facility. Most unchurched people don't feel comfortable going into a church building. How would you feel about going to a meeting in a Mormon temple or a Hindu shrine? Probably so uncomfortable that you would not go. For this reason the "Military Wives" group of First Baptist Church in Norfolk, Virginia meets in the Norfolk Public Library, even though there is plenty of meeting space in their church building. It is really necessary to use your church facilities? Should you meet in a psychologically safer environment, like a home, restaurant, library, or other neutral location? Remember, the church is not buildings, it's people. And "...where two or three come together in my name, there am I with them" (Mt. 18:20).

It is often possible to develop a partnership with one or more local organizations or businesses in a community. Depending on your target audience, you may find local hospitals, hobby shops, schools, retirement homes, restaurants, etc. that share an interest in your cause and are happy to host the group and help you publicize your activities. This, by itself, will go a long way toward increasing the number of unchurched people who attend.

Publicity ideas and other support is often available through national Christian organizations that specialize in a particular area of ministry. The West Conroe Baptist Church has 120 people from the church and community playing basketball each week. "This ministry began as a passion of one of our members," says John Moody. "We partner with Upward Basketball [www.upward.org], a national ministry that provides churches with guidance on youth soccer, basketball, cheering, and flag football."[4] Want to start a divorce-recovery Heartbeat ministry? Go to: www.DivorceCare.com. Passionate about starting a community garden Heartbeat ministry? See www.GrowingPower.org. Check www.HeartbeatMinistries.net for a growing list of resources, including national organizations, that are available.

LAND MINE #8: **Meaningful relationships are not developing among participants.**

Building relationships among participants in the new ministry is essential to developing community. Good ice-breaker activities will help people learn about each other. Knowing—and sharing—backgrounds, likes and dislikes, families, jobs, fears and joys builds trust and opens the door for letting people in to a more intimate understanding of who we are. What makes you happy? Anxious? What was your childhood like? ... are questions that will build empathy and trust.

Or, try eating together. There is something special that happens when we eat together. It creates a comfortable environment to relax, laugh, share, and bond. John Chandler, a long-time student of effective churches, observes that, "...

not all groups that grow eat together. But all groups that eat together seem to grow. It is my overwhelming experience that eating together is one of the best ways to build community."[5]

Members of the group should be encouraged to share special events in their lives: graduations...new babies...illness...job promotion/loss...health concerns... engagements...grandchildren. If a family member is sick or struggling, group prayer (even if it is only from the chaplain) will be greatly valued. These are opportunities for celebrating victories, and sharing sorrows. If the events are important to the individual, they should be important to the group.

Providing support is not just for Christians; anyone can empathize and encourage another. It goes on all the time in non-Christian circles. But adding Christian empathy and prayer to a situation gives a unique perspective of Christian faith, hope, and love to those who are not believers. One of the great values of a side-door group is having fellow travelers with whom to share some of life's journey. The common phrase is true: "People don't care how much you know, until they know how much you care."

The goal of every Heartbeat ministry is, at some point within the first year, to move beyond meeting just felt needs and include meeting deeper needs. Felt needs are not insignificant. A single mom with three kids has immediate and felt needs of time, health, finances, stress. Those needs are very real, and very pressing.

But after the felt needs are met, the deeper needs of the soul still yearn for solace. "The difference between real and felt needs is important to understand," note Conn & Ortiz. "The felt needs of poor people often deal with the physical – food, housing, transportation, medicine. However, the deeper, real need has to do with valuing themselves as creations of God, reclaiming the dignity God desires them to have and finding the hope of a transformed life in Christ."[6]

What are those deeper needs? We mentioned them earlier. People are looking for:

- ♦ a place to belong
- ♦ a sense of balance
- ♦ authentic relationships
- ♦ spiritual answers
- ♦ help through transitions

Rick Warren' gives his list of deeper needs:

- ♦ Support—Everyone wants to know they're not alone;
- ♦ Stability—People are looking for a strong foundation to build their life on;
- ♦ Self-Expression—People want an opportunity to express their uniqueness
- ♦ Significance—We all want to know that our life matters.[7]

Addressing people's deeper needs is an important purpose of a Heartbeat ministry. When people in the group become sensitive to, and then respond to, these needs you will see inter-personal bonding in a powerful way; regardless of whether they are Christians or non-Christians.

The Ministry Coach should encourage MPT members to help build and strengthen relationships among those involved in the Heartbeat group. There are five helpful guidelines for deepening relationships we covered in Chapter Ten. Remind the ministry leaders to teach and apply these guidelines in their activities:

1. Learn and Practice the Skills of Listening.
2. Deepen the Level of Communication.
3. Practice empathy.
4. Identify a Need in the Person's Life.

5. Respond with an Appropriate, Caring Gift.

If the new ministry is support-oriented, people's feelings and emotions will come out sooner than if the new ministry has a recreational focus. But in either case, intentional planning and time will build deeper relationships.

LAND MINE #9: Church attenders are not bonding with unchurched people in the group.
Be conscious of the social dynamics when the group is together. Do church members and non-members seem to be comfortable with each other? Are they enjoying the presence of each other's company? Or, do church members seem to cluster with other church member friends and ignore the non-members?

If you see such social segregation happening, group leaders should speak privately with the church people about it. Remind them that there are non-members in the group and it is important to go out of their way to involve everyone in conversation and activities. In your planning, intentionally pair members/non-members together for activities, ice-breakers, or projects. Encourage church members to plan extra-curricular activities and invite non-members in the group.

MINE FIELD #10: Unchurched people in the new ministry are not coming to worship.
If your church has only one worship service, and the service has not changed much over the past 40 years, ask yourself whether an unchurched person in your new ministry would really feel comfortable there. In many churches across America the services are honestly *not* very appealing to unchurched people. (Why do you think they're not coming in the first place!?) The "in-house" language, the welcome (or lack of it), the quality and content of the service is just

not attractive to people who aren't used to going to church. Of course, most church services are not designed for the unchurched; and that's fine. I'm not suggesting you change the entire format and focus of your worship service for the benefit of a small minority of unchurched people. So, what's my point?

I suggest that—in the first twelve months of a relationship with an unchurched person through your new ministry—it is not necessary that he/she be in your Sunday morning service. Of course, there is certainly nothing wrong if they do show up. And, if they do, they should be warmly welcomed. A friend from the ministry group should sit with them...introduce them to the pastor and friends in the church...invite them out to dinner afterwards. But, the process of coming to faith is one that takes time. And it is likely that attending a Sunday worship service, while important, will be later in a "pilgrim's progress," rather than earlier.

"Big events" at a church are great opportunities to invite new friends from the Heartbeat group. Christmas concerts, summer outings, mission trips. Most unchurched people will not go to a church-sponsored event if they aren't personally invited. But many will go if they are. I was in Little Rock, Arkansas recently where First Baptist Church just finished their first "HuntFest." The church is not extremely large by today's standards; 450 or so. But one of the members came up with the idea of a 6-hour gathering for hunters and their families. There were kids activities, a great meal, door prizes (including a new ATV). They sold over 1100 tickets (at $20 each!), and most were to unchurched friends and community members. The HuntFest provided members with a perfect opportunity to invite unchurched friends.

If you don't have the wherewithal to put on many big events, there are often Christian events going on near by. Perhaps a larger church or ministry organization is putting on a concert. A popular Christian speaker or author may be giving a talk across town. Even if you have to drive a few hours, or stay overnight, events like this are great ways to strengthen relationships and provide additional exposure to the Christian message.

LAND MINE #11: **People are not coming to Christian faith.**

"Once you have created a new side-door into your church," says Todd Pridemore, "it is important to think about how to most appropriately invite non-church members involved in that activity to consider becoming disciples of Jesus. Side-doors are often just the first of many steps in the process of making disciples."[8]

Here's a graphic showing the three kinds of need-meeting ministry in which a Heartbeat ministry should eventually address. This does not mean that when a group moves to the next level they abandon the previous one. It means that, over time, meeting additional kinds of needs should enlarge the purpose of the group.

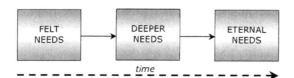

George Hunter, a student of church growth for over 30 years, alludes to these three steps in his new book, *The Apostolic Congregation*: "First, get in ministry with pre-Christian people, then get in conversation with them, then include God in the conversation."[9]

In the ultimate scheme of things, this is what it's all about. A personal faith in, and relationship with, Jesus Christ. Side-door ministries should help people experience the joy of life in Christ and in the body of Christ—a local church. As people outside the church develop meaningful connections with Christians, those friendships become the "bridges of God" for many people to experience God's love first hand. "I've never been able to persuade someone intellectually to abandon the relativistic mindset," says David Hill, on staff at Willow Creek's Axis ministry. "What's more likely to happen is that they'll see the power of a transformed life in another Christ-follower and be transformed."[10]

One of the great benefits of a side-door is that it provides a place where non-Christians can develop genuine and unconditional friendships with Christians. And the feeling is mutual. "Because compassion is core to our purpose," says Nathan Oates of Emmaus Church Community, "we seek to be a church community that goes to the people. We reach people by loving people. Individual transformation will fuel, and be fueled by, authentic expressions of Christian community."[11]

If all you do is good deeds, without introducing people to Christ, you are not focusing on the reason God sent his son: to seek and to save those who are lost (Luke 19:10), or our mandate to go and make disciples (Matthew 28:20). Christ's number one priority? To make disciples. So, how can you bring people closer to a relationship with Christ through a Heartbeat ministry? Here are some ideas...

✓ Appoint a chaplain. Every Heartbeat ministry, regardless of its purpose, should have one. The chaplain brings a relevant devotional thought and prayer at each gathering...circulates and delivers get-well cards to anyone in the group who is sick...prays for, sends flowers, or visits those in the group (and perhaps their friends or relatives) who may be in special need. The chaplain's purpose is to bring a spiritual ethos to the group and its activities.

✓ Provide times for spiritual exposure. Each Heartbeat ministry gathering should have a time where members are exposed (if even just briefly) to spiritual matters. Perhaps it is a short devotional by the chaplain or group leader. Maybe it is a story or article from the Internet with a spiritual perspective. It might be a reference to something from church the previous week, or a sermon series being given by the pastor. "Communication theorists partly explain attitude change and conversion by the 'cumulative effect' of many communications and experiences over time," notes George Hunter. "Willow Creek Community Church confirmed the theory and popularized the analogy of the 'chain of experiences.' Each experience adds a link in the chain that leads to faith and new life".[12]

✓ Create a spiritual culture. Here is an excerpt from an article in a secular Colorado Springs newspaper, reporting on the 250+ side-door sports and recreation ministries of First Presbyterian Church:

> Every event builds in a faith introduction. Church leaders want to get people through the church door. More than 39,000 people participate in First Presbyterian's Recreational Ministries every year, about 40% come from outside the church. Church officials want that percentage to go up. The ideal split, they say, is about 50-50, which allows unchurched folks to easily meet and form friendships with churchgoers. Those friendship create a base for spiritual growth.[13]

✓ Pray. It is quite appropriate for the chaplain to ask group members if they have any concerns or know people who need prayer. According to research, 81% of Americans pray[14]. And everyone has needs or concerns. The prayers need not be limited to the chaplain's utterances. Anyone in the group can pray; but no one should feel pressured, or uncomfortable if they don't. It has been my experience that non-Christians are more likely to ask for prayer for friends or family than for themselves. And, I believe God hears and answers the prayers of non-Christians.

Jim Engle has developed a helpful visualization of how and when people come to Christian faith. He calls it the "Spiritual Decision-Making Process."[15] This scale illustrates that conversion is really more of a process than an event, and that people progress through various stages in their faith journey. Bob Whitesel has summarized the Engle Scale and written an entire book elaborating on these "waypoints" in the Christian journey:[16]

The Spiritual Decision-Making Process

Level	Description
-11	No "God framework"
-10	Experience of emptiness
-9	Vague awareness and belief in God
-8	Wondering if God can be known
-7	Aware of Jesus
-6	Interested in Jesus
-5	Experience of Christian love
-4	Aware of the basic facts of the Gospel
-3	Aware of personal need
-2	Grasp the implications of the Gospel
-1	Challenged to respond personally

0	Repentance and faith
+1	Post-decision evaluation
+2	Functioning member of local church
+3	Conceptual and behavioral growth

The fact that people progress through steps in their Christian pilgrimage means that not every unbeliever who is involved in a Heartbeat ministry will be at the same place on their spiritual journey. Engle makes the important point that effective evangelism is helping people move forward *one step at a time*. It is a mistake (and research shows it is actually *counter*-productive to long-term discipleship) to expect people to go straight to "repentance and faith" ("0") regardless of where they may be on the Scale. If someone is at "Awareness of Jesus" (Stage -7), for example, effective evangelism strategy helps them become "Interested in Jesus" (Stage -6), then "Experience Christian Love" (Stage -5), etc..

But, regardless of where the person may be on the Engle Scale, over the course of their movement toward repentance and faith it is likely that conversations will touch on Christ and Christianity. "Loving acts and compassion are foundational to our witness," says Rebecca Pippert. "But if we never share the reason for our love, we run the risk of non-believers thinking we're simply Boy Scouts! As important as love is—it's not enough."[17] Scripture tells us: "Always be prepared to give an answer to everyone who asks you to give the reason for the hope that you have. But do this with gentleness and respect." (I Pe 3:15) So, what does a Christian say when the topic of "religion" comes up?

I have found the following four questions to be helpful in spiritual conversations. These questions—and their answers—should be the basis for a series of sermons, classes, or small group study in your church. When the subject of

Christian faith arises, church members should have thought about how they would answer these questions. It can also be helpful for members to share their answers with fellow believers for practice and feedback:

- How has being a Christian made a difference in my life?
- What does it mean to be a Christian (in words understandable to a non-Christian)?
- Why would I like my friend to be a Christian and member of my church?
- How does a person become a Christian (in words understandable to a non-Christian)?

Conclusion

I hope this chapter has not discouraged you from seeing the powerful possibilities of side-doors in your church. Realistic leaders know that a worthwhile task—or journey—will not be without its challenges. My purpose in this chapter has been to help you anticipate situations, and be prepared before the fact rather than unprepared after.

While there will certainly be obstacles along the way, the satisfaction you gain by helping Christians pursue their passion through a new ministry is one of the most fulfilling things you will ever do. That's because you'll be helping others to do one of the most fulfilling things they have ever done as a part of growing the body of Christ.

chapter seventeen

On Beyond Zebra

We have covered a lot. We have learned about a way to connect with people in your community, and hopefully be Christ-like (incarnational) in those relationships. We have learned that it really is possible for more people in your church to be involved in more outreach, doing more ministry, having more fun than anyone might have ever imagined. I hope we have provided some suggestions that will help you apply the idea of side-doors in your own church, in your own personalized way.

As we conclude, I want to leave you with a few mind-stretching ideas. These are ideas with a solid basis in reality. Because they are actually happening. We are seeing some Heartbeat ministries take amazing and exiting directions. So, with deference to one of my favorite Dr. Seuss books, let's peek into the future "on beyond Zebra…"

From a Heartbeat Ministry to a Signature Ministry

In some churches, what began as a group of people sharing a common interest or concern, has grown beyond their wildest imaginations. From a small gathering of passionate people, the ministry has mushroomed into a "Signature Ministry"—a ministry that has high visibility and influences a substantial number of people in the community.

"A signature ministry," Rev. L.D. Wood-Hull told his members at St. Barnabus Episcopal Church in Portland, "is when someone in our neighborhood discovers you belong to St. Barnabas, and she says, 'Oh, St. Barnabas—you're the ones who [fill in signature ministry here]'."[1]

A Signature ministry is often an "umbrella" of activities and services that are widely known in the community and define a significant part of the church's public identity. In some cases these ministries actually become independent, non-profit 501(c)(3) organizations with their own officers, budget, and facility. Then it really gets exciting!

The motorcycle ministry at Grove City Church of the Nazarene (Columbus, Ohio) began with a few young men getting together after church. It is now an independent ministry with its own name ("Gears"), its own website (www.gears-mm.org), a variety of special events and community service projects. The annual "Biker Weekend" of this church's Signature ministry has become the largest gathering of motorcyclists in the state of Ohio.

The Cancer Ministry of Snellville United Methodist Church (Snellville, Georgia) began in the heart of one member who lost a good friend to breast cancer. The experience motivated her into action, and today the services of this Signature ministry include client visitation, prayer teams, chemo buddies, child care, transportation, financial counseling, and meals on wheels. The ministry has been Christlike to over one thousand families in the last seven years.

The Washington Cathedral (Redmond, Washington) has spawned five non-profit ministries since its birth in 1984, all of which originally grew out of the passion of just a few people in the church. These Signature ministries include *Charity Alliance*, which focuses on giving to and empowering those most hurting in their community; the *Health Resource Center*, which sponsors 12-Step ministries, a counseling center, and medical clinics; *Excel Ministries* helps people discover that success in the marketplace is finding and fulfilling God's plan for their lives on an ethical pathway; *Washington*

Seminary, which offers four state-approved master's degrees and four different schools specializing in training lay people for excellence in lay ministry; and *Build the Family Center*, which specializes in working to make the world a safer place for children.

Affinity Churches, House Churches, and Beyond
Some of your Heartbeat ministries may even grow to become their own church! In fact, if your church offers only one service, on one day of the week, at one time of day, with one style of music, and one "clientele" of worshipper, then it would be to your church's benefit to encourage some of your stronger side-door ministries to become new churches. Ginghamsburg United Methodist Church (Dayton, Ohio) has, at last count, 23 different "specialized" churches in their ministry.

"House Churches" are growing rapidly across the country, as places that provide a genuine source of Christian caring and community. Some of your Heartbeat ministries may develop real momentum of unity and community, attracting many who would feel out of place in your existing church. If so, consider giving birth to a daughter church; a Heartbeat church!

Perhaps an "Affinity Church" is in the future of some of your Heartbeat ministries. Take the Church in the Wind, a Motorcycle Church in Denver, Colorado that holds its worship services "on the road". (Saves on building maintenance, I guess.) Or, the Church of the Joyful Healer, a Karate Church in McKinleyville, California that originally began as the heartbeat of one man to lose weight and lower his blood pressure. Or, the Happy Trails Cowboy Church in Taylorsville, North Carolina with services every Monday night in a local rodeo arena. (If anyone in your church has a honkerin' to rope them li'l doggies, there is a national Cowboy Church

Network—www.cowboychurch.net—that will be happy to help get you stated.)

"When people find somebody with the same passion they have," says Richard Harris of the Southern Baptist Home Mission Board, "they are interested, and attracted."[2] The Southern Baptist denomination started over 1,700 "Affinity Churches" in a recent year, including golf churches, blue grass churches, motorcycle churches, and lots of cowboy churches.

So, wherever your side-door journey takes you, my friend, I wish you well. Because there are exciting days ahead. I hope the ideas we have shared here have given you a sense of optimism, as well as direction, for what God can do in your church...how he can use the unique "snowflakes" in your congregation to bring others into his family and the fellowship of Christ's church. As you embark on your journey, remember the Old Testament story of Mordecai, who was desperately trying to save the Jewish people from destruction. The words he wrote to Queen Esther may be the words God is speaking to you and your congregation at this moment in time: *"Who knows but that you have been called to the kingdom for such a time as this"* (Esther 4:14).

epilogue

To conclude our time together I would like to share with you a true story. Yet, it is also a parable. It is a parable about the amazing potential for new ministry and outreach hidden beneath the surface in your congregation! The story illustrates how easily we can miss the potential God has given us, unless we learn to see what we are looking for...

- -

There was once a farmer who lived in the mountains of Africa. He owned a very large farm with orchards, grain fields, and gardens. He was a wealthy contented man. Contented because he was wealthy, and wealthy because he was contented!

One day a visitor came to his farm and described the fortunes being made by people discovering diamond mines. The visitor told in vivid detail of the beautiful stones looking like drops of "congealed sunlight." He described how a handful of diamonds could purchase any desire of the farmer's heart, and place his children on thrones around the world through the influence of his great wealth.

That night the farmer went to bed a poor man—poor because he was discontented, and discontented because he feared he was poor. As the farmer lay on his bed thinking of wealth, he said aloud: "I want a mine of diamonds." All night he lay awake thinking about diamonds. When morning came he sought out the stranger for directions to where these gleaming gems might be found.

"In white sands between high mountains," he was told.

"I will go!" said the farmer. So, he sold his farm, left his family with a neighbor, and went off in search of diamonds. He searched through mountains and valleys, through deserts and plains. For years and years he searched for diamonds. At last, when his money was spent and his clothes were in rags, wretched and ruined he stood on a bridge with swirling water below. That poor, afflicted, suffering man could not resist the awful temptation to cast himself into the water, where he sank beneath the dark surface, never to rise in this life again.

Some time later, the man who had purchased the farm was walking along the stream on his property. He happened to look down, and as he did, noticed a curious flash of light. The man reached down and picked up a dark colored stone, having an eye that beautifully reflected the colors of the rainbow. He took the curious stone into the house, left it on the mantle, and forgot about it.

Months later the same stranger returned. Upon entering the house he saw the flash of light from the stone on the mantle and rushed over to it. "This is a diamond!" he said. "This is a diamond!"

"No, no," said the owner, "that is not a diamond. It is just a stone I found out in my stream."

"It is a diamond," insisted the stranger.

Together they returned to the stream and stirred up the white sands with their fingers. There they found other, more beautiful, more valuable gems than the first. Thus was discovered the actual mine of Golconda, the most prolific diamond mine in the history of mankind.

The old farmer had owned literally acres of diamonds. For every acre—yes, every shovel-full from that old farm—contained the gleaming gems. Yet he had sold his land for practically nothing, in order to look for diamonds elsewhere. Had he only taken the time to know what diamonds look like in their rough state, and had he first explored his own land, he would have discovered more riches than he had ever imagined possible…right under his own feet!

This amazing, true story should remind us of a very real possibility. It is that each of us, at this very moment, may be standing on our own "acres of diamonds." Look again at your congregation…now with more educated eyes. Do you see flashes of light in those common stones? Do you see sparkles of potential value in the passions…joys…strengths…and experiences of your people? If you look closely, if you recognize those flashes of light in their rough state, they are diamonds.

Go ahead. Reach down. Pick some up. Break them loose from their confines. Hone them. Shape them. Because they hold the potential to bring more people to the throne of Jesus Christ and into the fellowship of your church than you ever imagined possible.

Look around. You are surrounded by "acres of diamonds."

Appendices

APPENDIX A

Congregational Survey

Thank you for taking a few moments to complete the following survey. The purpose for requesting this information is to develop a "personality profile" of our church family... to identify common ages, interests, concerns, marital status, family status, etc.. If you are a member or regular attender of our church, we would appreciate your taking time to complete and return this survey. As our church profile becomes clearer, we will share the information as we explore ways to be most effective in ministry to and through the Body of Christ.

Please complete one survey <u>per person</u> (13 yrs. and older).

Born in year:_____

Marital Status

    ❏ I am presently **single**   (please check one box below)
        ❏ never married
        ❏ divorced; # of years since most recent divorce:_____
        ❏ widow/er; # of years since most recent loss:_____
        ❏ other:_____

❏ I am presently **married** <small>(please check one box below)</small>
    ❏ 1st marriage; # of years married:_____
    ❏ 2nd marriage; # of years in present marriage:_____
    ❏ 3rd marriage; # of years in present marriage:_____

❏ I am presently **separated** # of months or years since separation:_____

Family Status <small>(check all that apply)</small>

❏ I have children living at our home
    - Please list birth year of each child:_____
❏ I have grandchildren living at our home
    - Please list birth year of each child:_____
❏ There are one or more children in our home are not *biologically* related to me ("blended family," adopted, legal custody, foster, etc.)
❏ I have grown children living out of the house
❏ I have some children grown and some still at home
    - Please list birth year of each child:_____
❏ I have never had children
❏ I have minor (biologically-related) children who are not living in my home

Special Interests

The hobbies I enjoy, and the approximate number of hours I spend with each hobby in an average month:

<u>Hobby</u>	<u>Approx. # hours/month</u>
_____	_____
_____	_____
_____	_____
_____	_____

Special Concerns

Beyond what might be considered "normal concerns," I feel particularly worried about:

❑ my marriage
❑ my children
❑ my parents
❑ my health
❑ my job
❑ my finances
❑ _____
❑ _____

Life Experiences

I have experienced the following events within the past five years. (check all that apply)

❑ Death of a spouse

❑ Change in number of arguments with spouse

❑ Divorce

❑ Took out a loan over $300,000

❑ Move to nursing/retirement home

❑ Foreclosure on a mortgage/loan

❑ Marital separation

❑ Significant feeling of not being wanted/needed

❑ Death of a close family member

❑ Outstanding personal achievement

❑ Major physical problems

❑ Spouse began or stopped work

❑ Marriage or remarriage

❑ Significant decrease in contact with children

❑ Void of personal life goals

❑ Dramatic change in personal behavior patterns

❑ Financial loss of retirement money

❑ Significant decrease in contact with friends

- ❑ Forced early retirement
- ❑ Loss of ability to drive
- ❑ Marital reconciliation
- ❑ Retirement
- ❑ Spouse confined to nursing home
- ❑ Change of health of family member
- ❑ Gain a new family member
- ❑ Significant change in financial condition
- ❑ Death of a close friend
- ❑ Difficulty in getting medical insurance

- ❑ Trouble with the boss
- ❑ Minor physical problems
- ❑ Significant change in recreational habits
- ❑ Significant change in church activities
- ❑ Significant change in social activities
- ❑ Took out a loan of less than $300,000
- ❑ Significant change in sleep habits
- ❑ Change in frequency of family get-togethers
- ❑ Significant change in eating habits
- ❑ Minor law violation

TALKING POINTS
Discussion Guide

Purpose of these questions:

You are reading these pages...because you have a heartbeat! Your physical heart, of course, is beating inside your body. But you also have an "emotional heart" beating inside your soul. It is your priorities, values, and passions that have been growing in you since birth. Your emotional heartbeat is what makes you...you.

The following questions will help you consider whether your emotional heartbeat—the passions God has created in you— might be the "seed" of a new group or ministry that could touch people with God's love! This brief conversation guide will 1) help you to think through such a possibility, and then 2) organize the discussion in an exploratory interview between you and your pastor or Ministry Coach.

Prior to the meeting please think about, and then write out, your responses to the questions below, and bring two copies to the meeting. These questions will help you clarify your thoughts, as well as give others a better likelihood of under-standing of your ideas, and perhaps even enhance these ideas for maximum ministry.

What's Your Dream?

1. In a few sentences, explain what kind of ministry you're thinking about:

2. Take a moment and envision what this ministry might look like five years from today (i.e., how many people are involved or touched by the ministry, what activities are occurring, etc.):

3. What past experiences (personally or professionally) have you had that qualify you in this area of ministry?

4. Do you know anyone (church members or otherwise) who might be interested in working with you to pursue this new ministry idea? Who are they and how do you know them?

What is the Need?

1. Who would be affected by—and benefit from—this ministry?

2. What other organizations/churches are you aware of that provide a related service or ministry...

    a) in our community?

    b) in other areas of the city or country?

What is the Opportunity?

A key part of considering new ministries in our church is the potential for connecting with, and reaching out to,

2

new and unchurched people. How do you see this occurring in this ministry?

What Will it Cost?

1. What kind of financial requirements and expenses do you anticipate (short-term & long-term)?

2. Can you think of some ways these expenses might be covered?

TO BE COMPLETED WITH
PASTOR/MINISTRY COACH

A "to-do" list of immediate next steps as a result of today's discussion:

Action Step	Person Responsible	By When

Planning Your Focus Group/s

The following responsibilities should be assigned to make your focus group/s a success:

- *FINDING A LOCATION* (person responsible):

  The ideal location is a neutral site designed to conduct focus groups. That is, the room is relatively small, it has a two-way mirror for observation, and a microphone/speaker so that the conversation can be monitored in the observation room. Such locations are often found in universities, counseling centers, and business complexes.

  If an ideal room cannot be located, the second choice would be in a neutral location with a secluded room, such as a restaurant, motel, school, or office. The disadvantage of not having a room with a two-way mirror is that it is more difficult for observers to be present and benefit from the conversation. Sometimes a video camera can be mounted in the room and used to view the session on a monitor in another room.

- *RECRUITING PARTICIPANTS* (person responsible):

  The ideal number of participants in a focus group is eight to twelve. Less than eight persons tends to cast doubt on the validity of the information obtained. More than twelve makes the focus group difficult to manage and have everyone participate.

  Participants should be selected because they are representative of your target group. The best way to invite participants is a telephone call or personal invitation if you know they qualify as being in the target audience. A newspaper ad, flyer, or mailing may get some participants, but your response rate will only be 1-2%, at best. Since it is likely only one of every two people who say they will attend the group actually show up, it is best to have 15-20 people signed up for each group.

  Remember that your target audience is not just Christians or church members. Don't take the easy way out and recruit your focus group only among church members. At least half of your focus group participants should be unchurched.

  People are most likely to accept an invitation to participate in a focus group if they are invited by a person they know. Church members can invite friends or relatives, explaining that their church is doing research on a certain target groups in the community and is looking for research participants. Most people (members and non-members) do not find such an invitation to be inappropriate or difficult.

All solicitations to participate in a focus group should include a phone number to call if they are interested, so that you can screen the possible participants. More people will volunteer if they are reimbursed $35 - $50 for their time.

- *LEADING THE FOCUS GROUP* (person responsible):

A focus group is somewhat similar to a group therapy session in that the purpose is to find out how participants feel about a particular issue in an open and accepting environment. There are no right or wrong answers. When a comment is made, the focus group leader may follow up with another question or a request for clarification. Or other members in the group may be asked about how they respond to the original comment. Thus, the focus group leader should be sensitive to the group interaction, and able to "bring out" the thoughts and feelings of people on related topics.

- *RECORDING THE FOCUS GROUP* (person responsible):

If the room in which you will be meeting is designed for focus groups, an audio or video recording system should be available. The microphone designed to carry the conversation into the observation room may also be jacked into a recorder. If this is the case, make arrangements prior to the day of the focus group to test the system and be sure you know how to operate it.

If you don't have access to such a room, or the room is not equipped with recording equipment, find a small tape recorder and place it on the table which the group is sitting around.

Be certain to test the equipment, batteries, microphone, etc. well before the meeting. Be sure that the microphone/s pick up the comments when group members are seated around the table. At the outset of the focus group participants should be made aware that the recorder is there only for the purpose of recording comments and allowing the focus group leader to concentrate on the conversation. Written permission should be obtained for the use of the recorder. If anyone strongly objects, don't use it. Very few, however, have a problem with it.

- *SUMMARIZING THE INFORMATION* (person responsible):

  Immediately following the focus group(s), the leader and observers should meet and debrief the session. (Observers may wish to make notes throughout the session, as well as during the discussion afterwards.) Try to develop some key generalizations from the session, particularly as it relates to your new ministry initiative.

- *PROVIDING REFRESHMENTS* (person responsible):

  Participants in the focus groups should be treated as guests. They will probably arrive prior to the starting time, so refreshments (coffee, doughnuts, cookies, etc.) are a nice touch. Refreshments may also be available during the focus group session.

- *INVITING OBSERVERS* (person responsible):

  If there are persons in the church who you feel would benefit from, or be interested in, observing the focus group, you may wish to invite them. Often times this can be an "eye-opening" experience for people who have difficulty believing that a new ministry is really what is needed. When these people hear comments from your "target group" their minds are often opened to new ideas.

Appendix D

"You Are Special" booklet

This 24-page booklet is an excellent way to spread the word among members that your church is in the "ministry mid-wife" business. It tells the story of common people who discovered a way to turn their interest outward...into a ministry. Readers of this booklet are encouraged to think about their own interests, concerns and passions, and consider whether God might be preparing them to start a new ministry. The booklet may be purchased in quantity at: www. HeartbeatMinistries.net, or by calling: 800-844-9286.

You are what you have been becoming... and God doesn't waste experience!

You Are Special! ...and God doesn't waste experience...especially yours!

"...all things work together for good to those who love God, to those who are called according to His purpose" (Romans 8:28).

Have you ever thought of yourself as a snowflake?

Twenty thousand feet above the earth moisture begins to concentrate. Molecules of hydrogen and oxygen condense. Small droplets of water materialize and begin falling to earth.

Snowflakes all start out the same...

At the beginning of their journey the little raindrops are spheres of water 2 mm in diameter with a similar composition and density. But as they encounter frigid air currents blowing up and down, back and forth, the droplets condense around microscopic dust particles in the atmosphere.

Then an amazing thing happens...

A transformation begins. The little raindrops start turning into ... snowflakes. They change at different times, speeds, and altitudes. But by the time each gently settles to earth, not one snowflake is the same as another. Their journey has transformed them.

Our lives are like snowflakes...

At the outset of our journey we all look about the same: tiny embryos only a few centimeters in diameter with the same composition and density. But then, at birth, we begin our unique journey. We encounter certain events, meet certain people ... develop certain attitudes. We experience love... pain... apathy...joy.

Your journey is transforming you...

Your previous experiences have shaped you. Some more than others. Perhaps you lost a parent in early childhood, or a child in early parenthood. Possibly you survived cancer, or are fighting to. Maybe it was abuse or divorce that highly influenced the snowflake you are today.

You are unique...

But, so what? What difference does it make that your life, your pain, your joys, and your passions are different than anyone else? The answer to that question is both simple, yet profound...

God doesn't waste experience!

Whoever you are, whatever you have been becoming, that unique person can be used by God—in a unique way—that only you and God can imagine.

Maybe, at this point, even you can't imagine...

But Scripture tells us, "...all things work together for good to those who love God, to those who are called according to His purpose." In that sense, God is not just talking about you...

He is talking TO you...

"I want to use your life, and your experiences, in a powerful way... if you will let me." God has been preparing you for something special... and only you can do it! Interested? Take the next step. Look up in the sky! Can you see it?

It's starting to snow!!!

Some real examples of how God is using "snowflakes".

The Least of These...

God doesn't waste experience.

Say Cheese

God doesn't waste experience.

22ng/ml

God doesn't waste experience.

Get a Life, Sister!

God doesn't waste experience.

What About You?

Has God given you a special interest, concern, or experience that could be the spark for a new ministry in our church? If you're thinking, "Maybe..." then here's the next step. Call our church office and ask for a copy of the DVD called, *Do We Have a Number?* It's just 30 minutes. But it could be a very important 30 minutes for you...for our church...and for people in our community.

Remember: **God doesn't waste experience!**

Introduction

1   John R.W. Stott, sermon delivered at the Keswick Convention July 17th 2007. http://www.langhampartnership.org/2007/08/06/john-stot-address-at-keswick/

2   John R.W. Stott, ibid.

3   http://en.wikipedia.org/wiki/Silver_bullet

4   Michael Anthony, "Testing the Research: Do People Still Come Through Relationships?" Presentation to American Society for Church Growth, Nov. 14, 2008, Talbot Seminary, La Mirada, California.

5   Tom Mercer, Oikos, Your World, Delivered. Chapel Hill, NC: Professional Press, 2009, p. 17.

6   Michael Green, Evangelism in the Early Church. Grand Rapids: Eerdmanns, 1970, p. 210.

7   Donald McGavran, Bridges of God: A Study in the Strategy of Missions. London: World Dominion Press, 1955

8   Anthony, op.cit.

9   Arn, Win & Charles, The Master's Plan for Making Disciples. Grand Rapids, MI: Baker Book House, 1998, p. 81.

10   Donald McGavran, Understanding Church Growth. Grand Rapids: William B. Eerdmans, 1990, Third edition. p. 209.

11   George Hunter, The Apostolic Congregation: Church Growth Reconceived for a New Generation, Nashville: Abingdon Press, p. 62.

Chapter One

1   George Hunter, Apostolic Congregations. Nashville: Abingdon Press, 2010, p. 62.

2   George Hunter, To Spread the Power: Church Growth in the Wesleyan Spirit, Abingdon, 1987, p. 79.

3   Kwasi Kena, "Offering Christ Today: Church Growth — Priority One, Be Fruitful" in EVANGELISM online newsletter. http://www.gbod.org/evangelism/articles.asp?item_id=14569, 2005.

⁴   Lyle Schaller, "How to Attract New People" in BuildingChurchLeaders.com/downloads/practicalministryskills/cultivatingactivechurchmembers/pl07-a.html

⁵   Gary McIntosh, Beyond the First Visit. Grand Rapids, MI: Baker Books, 2006, p. 22.

⁶   Denver Seminary Magazine: Fall 2004 Sep 15, 2004 Emergent Dialogue

⁷   Alan Roxburgh & Fred Romanuk, The Missional Leader. San Francisco: Jossey-Bass, 2006, p. xv.

⁸   George Hunter, The Apostolic Congregation Nashville: Abingdon, 2009, p. 116.

⁹   David Williamson, "Eight ways to reach out to the community through small groups." http://legacy.pastors.com/rwmt/article.asp?ArtID=11361.

¹⁰   George Hunter, The Apostolic Congregation. Nashville: Abingdon, 2009, p. 115

¹¹   Lee Sparks, "The State of Volunteer Ministry" REV! Jan/Feb. 2009, p. 52.

¹²   "Solving the Problem of Motivation," The Win Arn Growth Report, vol. 25.

¹³   Hunter, op.cit, p. 62

¹⁴   Donald McGavran, Understanding Church Growth. Grand Rapids: Eerdmans, 1980, P. 53.

¹⁵   Donald McGavran, Comment in "How to Grow a Church," 16mm film, Monrovia, CA: Church Growth, Inc., 1976.

¹⁶   Win & Charles Arn, The Church Growth Ratio Book. Pasadena: Church Growth Press. 2002, p. 26

¹⁷   Center Grove Presbyterian Church http://www.centergrove.org/outreach.htm

¹⁸   Lynn Fonfara, "What is the best method of evangelism?" in *Together*, June, 2007, p. 3.

¹⁹   Rick Warren, The Purpose Driven Church, Grand Rapids, MI: Zondervan Publishers, 1995, p. 326.

²⁰   http://www.fourthchurch.org/garden.html

²¹   Ray Bowman, When Not to Build. Grand Rapids: Baker Books, 2000, p. 32.

²²   Don Cousins, "Laying a Firm Foundation" wwwBuildingchurchleaders.com 208, CTI p. 46.

Chapter Two

[1] How to Grow a Church 16mm film Monrovia, CA: Church Growth, Inc., 1973.

[2] http://www.stchristophers-mn.org/outreach.htm#none

[3] Ted Haggard, Fly Fishing, Dog Training, and Sharing Christ in the 21st Century, Nashville: Thomas Nelson 2002, p. 11.

[4] C.S. Lewis, The Four Loves. Harcourt, Brace & Company, Orlando, FL, 1988, p. 247

[5] Stanley Mooneyham, in Who Cares About Love, Monrovia, CA: Church Growth Press, 1986, p. 104.

[6] http://letsbuildabridge.com/note-from-Andy.pdf

[7] http://everydayliturgy.com/being-missional-build-a-five-million-dollar-bridge/

[8] Rick Warren, "Explosive Growth: Unleash the Creativity of Your Congregation" Ministry Toolbox, #193."

[9] Flavil Yeakley, "Persuasion in Religious Influence" Chicago: University of Illinois, 1971, p. 148.

[10] David Stark, *Growing People through Small Groups* David Stark Bethany Press, 2004, p. 94.

Chapter Three

[1] Pam Heaton, "Every Church Needs a Profiler" at www.BuildingChurchLeaders.com

[2] Rick Warren, "Explosive Growth: Unleash the Creativity of Your Congregation" Ministry Toolbox #193.

Chapter Four

[1] George Hunter, The Apostolic Congregation. Nashville: Abingdon 2009, p. 115.

Chapter Five

[1] Win & Charles Arn, The Church Growth Ratio Book. Pasadena: Church Growth Press, 2001. P. 10.

2   "Turn the Church Inside Out" in Becoming Outward Focused series at BuildingChurchLeaders.com Christianity Today, 2000.

3   Thomas Holmes & R. Rahe, "The Social Readjustment Scale, The Journal of Psychosomatic Research 2, Elsevier Science Inc., 213-18, 1967.

4   ChurchMarketingSucks.com June 28, 2005.

5   *You Are Special* booklet is available for individual or quantity purchase from Heartbeat Ministries, www.HeartbeatMinistries.net or 800-844-9286.

6   Rick Warren, "Put People into ministry, not on committees" Ministry Toolbox, #186, Dec. 22, 2004, p. 1.

7   Alan Nelson, From Me to We. Loveland, CO: Group Publishing, 2007, p. 16.

8   Don Cousins, "Laying a Firm Foundation" in www. BuildingChurchLeaders.com/downloads/practicalministryskills/ startinganewministry/ps46-f.html

9   Ted Haggard, Fly Fishing, Dog Training, and Sharing Christ in the 21st Century, Nashville: Thomas Nelson, Inc., 2002, p. 5.

10   Haggard, op.cit., p. 5.

Chapter Eight

1   Mark Howell, "Five Keys to building a small groups ministry in a small to medium-sized church" Pastors.com/Ministry Toolbox.

2   Leith Anderson, Dying for Change. Minneapolis: Augsburg: Bethany Press, 1990; p. 99.

3   Wikipedia, http://en.wikipedia.org/wiki/Focus_group.

Chapter Nine

1   Todd Pridemore, "Does Your Church Have Side-doors?" in Net Results, Sept./Oct. 2004 p. 7.

Chapter Ten

1   http:insidechurch.blogspot.com/2007/03/Friday-night-dinner-club. html.

2   Bob Bast, Attracting New Members. Monrovia: Church Growth Press, p. 67-68.

3   Charles Arn, Who Cares About Love? Monrovia: Church Growth Press. Available by calling 800-844-9286 or online at: www. ChurchGrowth.net.

4   *Growing in Love* is available from Church Growth, Inc. (800-844-9286). It is also available online at: http://churchgrowth.net/products/audio/growinlove.htm.

5   Stanley Mooneyham, in *Who Cares About Love?* by Charles & Win Arn, Pasadena: Church Growth Press, 1992, p. 104.

6   Michael Johnson, "The 12 Mistakes of Christmas Outreach" http:// www.breakthroughchurch.com/12mistakes/12mistakes.html#10.

Chapter Fifteen

1   Alan Nelson, From Me to We, p. 16.

2   Todd Pridemoor, "Does Your Church Have Side-Doors?" in Net Results magazine, Sept/Oct 2004 p. 7.

3   You can download a .pdf file of this manual at www. HeartbeatMinistries.net. Printed, bound copies are also available from the same source.

4   Todd Pridemore, "Does Your Church Have Side-Doors?" *NET RESULTS Magazine September/October 2004, Vol. XXV, No. 5.*

5   Charles Arn, "You Are Special," Monrovia, CA: Heartbeat Ministries 2010, p. 10.

6   Pump-N-Praise brochure, published by Wheaton Bible Church, Wheaton, IL.

7   Flavil Yeakley, Why Churches Grow. Arcada, CO: Christian Communications, 1987, p. 44.

8   Flavil Yeakley, Persuasion in Religious Influence. Doctoral dissertation, University of Illinois, 1989, p. 142.

9   Mark L. Knapp & Anita L. Vangelisti. Interpersonal Communication and Human Relationships Boston: Allyn & Bacon, Inc. 2008.

10   Lyle Schaller, "How to Attract New People" in BuildingChurchLeaders.com/downloads/practicalministryskills/ cultivatingactivechurchmembers/pl07-a.html.

Chapter Sixteen

1   http://www.gisdevelopment.net/news/viewn.asp?id=GIS:N_lifd-vcuasz GIS Development (name of website) "...If only a map existed...Nazi mines stop Egypt's oil flow" 20 March 2008.

2   Rick Warren, "Explosive Growth: Unleash the Creativity of Your Congregation" in Ministry Toolbox #193.

3   Lyle Schaller, "How to Attract New People" in BuildingChurchLeaders.com/downloads/practicalministryskills/cultivatingactivechurchmembers/pl07-a.html

4   Krista Petty, "How Externally Focused Churches Minister to Children" Leadership Network white paper p. 7.

5   John Chandler, "3 Minutes" April 16, 2009 RASNET www.rasnet.org.

6   Harvie Conn and Manuel Ortiz, Urban Ministry, Downers Grove, IL: Intervarsity Press, 2001, p. 291.

7   Rick Warren, "Meeting People's Four Deepest Needs" in Ministry Toolbox #366 11/26/2008.

8   Todd Pridemore, "Does Your Church Have Side-Doors?" in Net Results magazine, Sept/Oct, p. 7.

9   George Hunter, *Apostolic Congregations*, Abingdon Press, 2010.

10 Bret Lawrence, "Starbucks Spirituality." www.ChristianToday.com/biblestudies/areas/biblestudies/articles/070815.html

11 Nathan Oates, "Growing Christian Community Through Relational Evangelism and Discipleship" in Grow Magazine, Winter, 2008 http://www.growmagazine.org/archive/winter2008/story_growing.html

12 George Hunter, The Apostolic Congregation, p. 117

13 The Gazette, Dec. 11, 2005 article by Paul Assay.

14 Cecil Maranville, "Flash: Americans Believe in Prayer!" in World News & Prophesy, January, 2004. http://www.wnponline.org/wnp/wnp0401/believeprayer.htm

15 James Engle, What's Gone Wrong With the Harvest? Grand Rapids, MI: Zondervan Publishing House, 1975.

16 Bob Whitesel, Spiritual Waypoints. Indianapolis: Wesley Publishing House, 2010.

17 Lindy Lowry, "God Came Down: An Interview with Rebecca Manley Pippert" Outreach magazine March/April, 2006, p. 35.

Chapter Seventeen

1   L.D. Wood-Hull, "A Signature Ministry for St. Barnabus" in: THE MESSENGER, Oct. 2008, p. 1 St. Barnabus Episcopal Church, 2201 SW Vermont St. Portland, OR

2   Laura Johnston Southeast Missourian online, "Southern Baptist 'affinity churches' tap niches to add members" Saturday, June 18, 2005 http://semissourian.rustcom.net/story/1106160.html.

CPSIA information can be obtained at www.ICGtesting.com
Printed in the USA
LVOW08s1156280914

406243LV00019B/386/P

9 781612 150536